Why Bother with the Bible?

Why Bother with the Bible?
Understanding the Book of Faith

C. Welton Gaddy

Judson Press ® Valley Forge

Why Bother with the Bible? Understanding the Book of Faith
© 1998 Judson Press, Valley Forge, PA 19482-0851

Library of Congress Cataloging-in-Publication Data
Gaddy, C. Welton.
    Why bother with the Bible? : understanding the book of faith / C. Welton Gaddy.
        p. cm.
    ISBN 0-8170-1262-1 (pbk.)
    1. Bible—Introductions. I. Title.
BS475.2.G33 1998
220.1—dc21   97-31508

Printed in the U.S.A.
05 04 03 02 01 00 99 98
5 4 3 2 1

Contents

Introduction

The Bible has been an important part of my life for as long as I can remember. "I pledge allegiance to the Bible . . ." For eight to ten days during every summer of my childhood, I repeated those words with my left hand raised high in the air and my right hand pressed tightly over my heart. That old Vacation Bible School ritual signaled a devotion to the Scriptures that influenced every facet of my young life year-round.

Many of my earliest and most pleasant memories cluster around the Bible: listening to my mother reading aloud a passage from the Bible every evening at bedtime; participating in "sword drills" ("Attention. Draw Swords. Charge!" the Bible drill leader barked like a military drill sergeant), in which the child finding an announced biblical passage the fastest received recognition; memorizing books of the Bible in their proper sequence; singing in a booster choir, "The B-I-B-L-E, yes that's the book for me. I'll stand alone on the Word of God, the B-I-B-L-E."

With increasing age came questions. The Bible held no exemption from them. Unfortunately, my home church did not welcome serious inquiries about the Scriptures. Even within the safety of my home, questions about the Bible often caused quite a stir. "Why is the Bible different from other books, and how? Did Jesus actually expect us to cut off one of our hands if we did something wrong with it? How can God be so vicious early in the Bible and so insistent on peace later?" I wanted to know.

College provided an opportunity for me to study the Bible as never before. Under the tutelage of scholarly, sensitive teachers, I felt biblical narratives come alive, discovering in the process that the Bible is not a compendium of doctrines or a code of ethics, as I earlier had imagined, but a lively book of diverse materials written by people of faith for people of faith and people in search of faith. Quickly I realized that an ancient text often provides the best possible counsel for dealing with a contemporary situation. My appreciation for the Bible expanded. Simultaneously, my faith grew by leaps and bounds.

Many of my older friends in our home church feared an academic study of the Bible. Misunderstanding a historical critical examination of the Bible, they equated *critical* with negative and made *literary investigation* synonymous with a lack of spiritual reverence. Just days before I left home to begin my seminary education, a well-intentioned pastor in the community warned me that studying the Bible in a seminary could "ruin" me.

My seminary experience ran directly counter to the sense of my friend's caution. The more seriously I studied the Bible, the more authority the Bible exerted over my life. Learning biblical languages opened new vistas into faith and truth. Careful analyses of biblical literature produced greater understanding and increased challenges to obedience. Asking hard questions about the Bible led to inspiring discoveries that deepened my personal devotion.

Recent years have brought to many people, including me, tidal waves of grief set in motion by cyclonic winds of controversy swirling around the Bible. Friends have parted company, congregations have divided, and denominations have fragmented because not everyone could endorse certain descriptive statements about the Scriptures. Stormy debates over how best to describe the Bible distracted debaters from pondering how the Bible describes itself. A near paranoid concern for what people should say about the Bible produced deafness to what the Bible says about people.

Much of the controversy over the Bible that has adversely affected local congregations in the last two decades probably could have been avoided had seminary-trained leaders in those churches consistently been more honest when teaching and preaching the Bible. Many ministers refused to acknowledge basic questions and predictable doubts related to the Scriptures, arguing that people in the pews were not equipped to handle the results of serious biblical study. Then, when major discussions about the Bible vaulted into national attention (often more as political footballs than as theological discussions), local congregations were ill equipped to listen and respond discerningly. Casualties of this situation often included congregational unity and even, in some instances, the commitment of individuals to thoughtful Bible study.

The resolve of American Baptist Churches in the U.S.A. to emphasize the importance of Bible study and Judson Press's production of materials to support that resolve merit commendation. I am delighted to participate in this important effort. What follows in this little volume is an experiential approach to the Bible—one person's approach to Bible study that perhaps can prove helpful to other people as well.

I have chosen to write in a rather casual, at points almost conversational, style. My ideas and terms to express them have taken shape while imagining readers (you) sitting in front of me, perusing an open Bible, raising questions, and chatting about common areas of interest. Though I have relied heavily on the careful studies of numerous scriptural scholars, I have tried to convey beneficial insights from their academic pursuits apart from a dependence upon technical language. Short of an opportunity to enjoy relaxed, face-to-face dialogue with each reader, I am sharing my thoughts about the Bible and telling my own personal story in relation to the Bible through this medium with a sincere hope that my work will prompt its readers to reflect on their own pilgrimages in relation to the Bible and affirm their beliefs about the Bible.

At the heart of this project pulses a desire to enable an approach to the Bible and an openness before the Bible that allow God's Word to challenge, inspire, and guide our lives, individually and socially. All of my words about *the* Word arise out of a prayer to God embracing the hope that God's Word will become flesh again as those of us who study the Bible live faithfully by it.

CHAPTER 1

Why Bother with the Bible?

I packed only a few items preparing to leave home for college. My mother asked if I planned to take my Bible to school. I honestly do not remember my intentions—whether or not I had decided to pack my Bible or if I even had thought about it. I do remember, though, the guilt that filled me in the aftermath of my mother's question. I did not have my Bible in my luggage. At the same time, embarrassment seeped into my emotions as I tried to anticipate what new acquaintances would think of a young man who brought a Bible with him to college. More guilt followed.

My mother's question sprang from her unshakable conviction about the importance of the Bible and its worthiness to receive time-consuming attention. Where I was going and what I would be doing did not alter her opinion. Never mind the scores of other books assigned for reading during my first semester. I had better read the Bible regularly, or so my mother thought. Was she right? How important is the Bible?

Bookstores bulge with volumes that vie with the Bible for the public's attention. Many of these popular books claim insights and venture predictions not found in the Bible. Some best-selling authors boast of personal life experiences considered superior to the truths of biblical narratives. A whole genre of self-help books pleads for readers' allegiance to normative principles and conformity to social strategies that find no support in the Scriptures. "Our programs work," their authors argue. So, why bother with the Bible?

From time to time, questions about the importance of the Bible even appear within churches. "Why can't we devote more time to nonbiblical literature in our educational programs and worship services?" an interested member of a parish inquires. "Why do we read three different passages of Scripture in a worship service?" someone else chimes in, "Isn't that a little much?" True, the church places great emphasis on the Bible—building worship experiences on the foundation of biblical texts, encouraging people to read the Bible daily, and systematically teaching the Bible to people of all ages. Why? Why cannot mature adults make up their own minds about matters without scurrying to search for the Bible's direction on every single issue? Why bother with the Bible?

Promises of the Bible

The Bible makes profound promises. Better stated, God makes profound promises through the Bible. Students of the Bible discover these promises as well as the power that brings them to fulfillment. Take 2 Timothy 3:16, for example. The author of this passage succinctly stated the Bible's value: "All Scripture is inspired by God and profitable for teaching, for reproof, for correction, and for training in righteousness, that the man [and woman] of God may be complete, equipped for every good work." Though the writer intended for his words to describe the importance of the Hebrew Scriptures (the New Testament did not yet exist), his comments apply equally well to the whole of the Bible as we now have it. The promises of 2 Timothy 3:16 underscore the worth of the biblical text. Ponder each of these promises, and you will begin to understand why Bible study is worth the effort.

The Bible Teaches

In the 2 Timothy passage, the sense of the word *teach* encompasses far more than take-it-or-leave-it lessons. A binding power pervades the instruction of God's biblical revelation. The message of the Holy Scriptures carries authority. We cannot disregard the teaching of the Bible, remain passive about learning biblical truths, apart from robbing ourselves of fundamental insights about the nature and meaning of life.

The Bible teaches us about the source of the world and our lives in it, the scandal of sin that adversely affects both, and the means by which God can overcome sin and establish reconciliation within creation.

The Bible teaches the significance of caring personal relationships in which individuals practice honesty, work at understanding, extend forgiveness, and share each other's joys and sorrows.

The Bible teaches who Christ is, how and why any individual can meet him in faith, and the nature of a life shaped by obedience to his teachings and conformity to his activities.

The Bible teaches the importance of a covenant community and criteria to be heeded when selecting leaders for it.

The Bible teaches us how to look to the past with faith, ponder the future with hope, relate to the present with love, and establish the highest priority among faith, hope, and love.

The Bible teaches us about spiritual growth—how to progress from a crawling, stammering, simplistic stage of spiritual infancy to the boldness, certainty, and in-depth convictions of spiritual maturity.

The Bible teaches us how to learn from an unassuming child who thinks everybody should be loved as well as from an aging adult who knows how difficult it is to really love anybody.

The Bible teaches us how to resolve anxiety, cope with pain, grow in suffering, find comfort in the face of death, and generally live with a peace that passes all understanding.

The Bible teaches the nature of evil and how it may be defeated as well as the essence of goodness and how it may be supported.

The Bible teaches the manner in which divinely acceptable worship finds expression corporately and individually, publicly and privately.

The Bible teaches us how to offer an influential witness to Jesus Christ through the words of our mouths, the meditations of our hearts, the thoughts of our minds, and the actions of our lives.

The Bible teaches.

The Bible Reproves

The word *reprove* has a negative ring to it. Subsequently, reproof often gets a bad rap. That is a shame. Actually, reproof is far from a restrictive gesture born of a negative attitude about life. Biblical reproofs bear evidence of divine compassion. Through the Bible, God seeks to stop us short when we are about to make serious errors, attempts to steer us away from harmful situations and help us avoid damaging decisions and destructive actions. Take a look:

The Bible reproves any attempt to replace the entirety of the biblical message with an emphasis on only one part of it.

The Bible reproves individuals who thoughtlessly chase after every novel interpretation of Scripture that comes along or spastically jump from one popular religious movement to another trying to guarantee that belief will always be simple, discipleship easy, and ministry successful.

The Bible reproves people who so vigorously seek popularity for the church, acceptance for the Word of God, and commendation for personal services that they compromise the authentic nature of all three.

The Bible reproves both individuals who substitute involvement in works of faith for faith itself and individuals who glory in their possession of faith apart from participation in works of faith.

The Bible reproves believers who establish their experience of faith as normative for everyone else and attempt, in relation to others, an exercise of comprehensive judgment that belongs to God alone.

The Bible reproves the irrelevant communication of simple solutions when complex problems demand an answer, the announcement of an appeasing message that may be desired when a prophetic proclamation is needed, and the declaration of an insight from the world when someone has requested a word from God.

The Bible reproves the thought that feeling good is synonymous with doing good.

The Bible reproves cockeyed optimism divorced from reality as well as cynical negativism devoid of promise.

The Bible reproves an obsession with success, which destroys a person's sense of obligation to God, family, friends, and other people.

The Bible reproves.

The Bible Corrects

Notice that in 2 Timothy's sequence of promises, "correction" stands between "reproof" and "training in righteousness." Correction comes at the midpoint of a person's pilgrimage from living in error (or sin) to learning what is right and living accordingly. God alone provides the correction that prepares people for an orientation to righteousness. That gift—God's correction—is available to everybody in the biblical revelation.

The Bible corrects people who confuse acknowledging God with serving God and mistake calling the name of Jesus for following the life of Jesus.

The Bible corrects misunderstandings of freedom that allow the benefits of liberty to be accepted and enjoyed without the responsibilities of liberty being assumed and performed.

The Bible corrects a philosophy that promises sin can be totally private and that predicts sin has no significant consequences.

The Bible corrects a preoccupation with Christ's second coming that diverts attention from the demands of his first coming.

The Bible corrects a pursuit of discipleship devoid of discipline and vision.

The Bible corrects a quantitative mentality that measures all progress numerically and ignores qualitative questions essential to responsible morality.

The Bible corrects affirmations of Jesus' greatness as prophet, teacher, and minister that stop short of an acceptance of Jesus as Savior.

The Bible corrects a legalism that distorts liberty and a libertinism that destroys life.

The Bible corrects proclamations that portray the gospel as a demand rather than a gift or suggest gospel-shaped obedience can occur without cost.

The Bible corrects self-appointed defenders of the faith who measure the orthodoxy of others by the criteria of doctrinal similarity and personal compatibility.

The Bible corrects attitudes fascinated with judgment and turned off by mercy.

The Bible corrects individuals who claim to love Christ while harboring disdain for his followers.

The Bible corrects theologies that identify Jesus as a man with no dimension of divinity or as a god with little more than the appearance of a similarity to humankind.

The Bible corrects moralities that equate what is natural with what is right or what is unnatural with what is good.

The Bible corrects troublers of the good in the body of Christ who live at peace with the evils of the world and individuals in both realms who avoid trouble at all costs to maintain peace at any price.

The Bible corrects.

The Bible Trains in Righteousness

Training is education, but more than the mind is involved. The Bible educates the whole person, affecting emotions as well as intellect, influencing actions as well as decisions. As a result of being trained by the Bible, people grow, progress, to the point that righteousness becomes a way of life. An individual trained in righteousness not only believes right but lives right, demonstrating conduct indicative of a child of God.

The Bible nurtures a consistency in personal thoughts, words, and deeds that constitutes a wholeness otherwise known as *integrity.*

The Bible instills within us a passion for truth, which breeds a practice of honesty.

The Bible sensitizes us to the needs of others and equips us to translate that sensitivity into needs-oriented ministry.

The Bible defines greatness in terms of service and identifies service as an act of love.

The Bible exalts peacemaking over violence, fidelity over unfaithfulness, commitment over self-indulgence, and grace over judgment.

The Bible commends the practice of true piety in the streets of communities as well as in the pews of church buildings.

The Bible summons people to serve God through their daily labor whether their work is secular or religious.

The Bible invites a responsible stewardship of time, money, talents, and natural resources, identifying such stewardship as obedience to God.

The Bible exemplifies and encourages a boldness in faith that finds delight and increased strength in doing right.

The Bible directs our vision beyond popular perception, peer-group pressures, and a potential for social acceptance or rejection in determinations of what is good.

The Bible instills within us an ability to face both life and death apart from destructive anxiety.

The Bible promotes interpersonal relationships that transcend racial, economic, social, and intellectual compatibility.

The Bible establishes justice as the bare minimum in our reactions to other persons and relentlessly presses for the primacy of grace.

The Bible elicits compassion characterized by a capacity to share good times and bad, to set limits and celebrate freedom, to insist on righteousness and offer forgiveness, and to praise health while working to heal illnesses.

The Bible integrates spiritual citizenship in the realm of God's rule with political citizenship amid the governments of this world.

The Bible calls us to a pilgrimage of faith on which fidelity to the journey is inseparable from the joy of arrival at its destination.

The Bible trains in righteousness.

A Complete Person

The purpose of the Bible is to produce a complete person, an individual of integrity. Responding positively to the ministry of the Bible results in a personal relationship with God. Taught, corrected, reproved, and trained by the Bible, a person receives the blessing of God's gift of salvation and accepts the responsibility to bless others in God's name. This individual models obedience to Jesus' mandate for wholeness—the meaning of the Greek word also translated as "perfect." Both wholeness and perfection carry the sense of the word "integrity"(Matthew 5:48). Beliefs and behavior square with each other. Internal convictions find social expression. Faith acts in love. Devotion to God leads to service to people in the world.

Provisions of the Bible

While the Bible opens our minds and spirits to what can be, this amazing book also enables us to see what is and provides us with the means for claiming God's abiding promises now. Honest personal engagements with the Bible allow Scripture writers to instruct us in the way of faith. Growing in appreciation for our predecessors in the faith and discovering hope as the perspective with which to view the future, we come to praise the Bible for assisting us in coping with the present.

A Book of Narration

The Bible tells us who we are, relating stories that mirror our experiences and give meaning to our lives. In a stage play by August Wilhelm von Schlegel, the curtain rises to show the inside of a theater where another audience sits waiting for a curtain to rise and a performance to begin. When that curtain goes up, yet another audience appears, this one also waiting for a curtain to rise. After a third repetition of this scene, members of the original audience grow uneasy. Many of them squirm in their seats and look back over their shoulders to see if perhaps they too are on stage. Von Schlegel's dramatic theatrical opening captures the sensation often experienced by people engrossed in reading biblical narration. The Bible's stories of people from a distant past extend into the present. Twists and turns of unfolding plots fill readers with a sense of "being there," at times as participants and at times as onlookers in these happenings.

Reading the Bible is like looking into a mirror. The stories in the Bible are our stories. Adam and Eve might as well be our names. Their sin is our sin, and their fall our fall. We rebel against God and turn our backs on grace only to have God come searching for us. Elijah had no corner on self-pity or even depression. We have been there. Though we may change the names to protect the guilty, David's infidelity pricks our consciences about betrayals in which we have been involved. Then, God's further use of David incites fierce hope about our futures.

Every time I read the Passion stories of the New Testament, I see my face in the crowd and identify character traits of my own reflecting off the leading figures in those narratives. Like the fickleness of those who lined the road when Jesus entered Jerusalem, I fluctuate in my faith between shouts of "Hosanna" and sentiments that crucify. Judas makes me inquire about the price tag attached to my devotion. Much later, after the light of the Resurrection has dawned amid the darkness that surrounded the Crucifixion, I realize that Jesus joins my journey in the very same way he showed up among the two travelers plodding toward Emmaus.

Some people have trouble with the apostle Paul. Could it be because the man from Tarsus demonstrated all the ambivalence and inconsistencies they (we) embody? Read his works. Like us, Paul affirms grace and struggles with law, praises equality and battles prejudice, tries to focus on Christ and has trouble shaking a preoccupation with personal difficulties.

I often think of the Bible as a religious counterpart to Chaucer's *Canterbury Tales.* In the Scriptures, we encounter personal stories drawn from myriads of experiences in a vast array of places over hundreds of years. Pilgrims detail events in which they met God, sinned, encountered mercy, discovered faith, laughed, cried, and worshiped. They speak to each other and about each other, to us and about us. While listening to the voices and pondering the tales these fellow travelers tell, we hear the voice behind all other voices and confront the source of all words and stories.

A Book of Illumination

The Bible reveals the nature of God, reporting and interpreting God's activities throughout history. Revelation consists of two components: an event plus an interpretation of that event. Learning from a revelation is like breaking out in laughter after getting the point of a good joke or suddenly exclaiming right in the middle of a lecture, "Oh, I see." A truth not previously known becomes apparent and understood.

Scholars often refer to the Bible as the book of the mighty acts of God. It is that. Please understand, though, that assertion is a declaration of faith. Some people label as freak events of nature, happenchance accidents, or outcroppings of sheer luck the very events that other people ascribe to the power of God. These persons who wrote the Bible were people of faith. Thus, they described various historical occurrences as acts of God and interpreted those acts with reference to the nature of God. Subsequently, readers of the Scriptures gain new understandings of God and develop their own in-depth faith in God. Revelation!

The Bible's accounts of God's past involvements in history prod us to consider how God presently shows up in our lives. Eventually, or suddenly, we see. God comes to us when we are sorely pressed by people we consider our enemies, just as God visited Daniel in a den of lions. God takes up residence in our midst when we are homesick, lonely, depressed, or preoccupied with a need, just as God walked with Ezekiel amid the hurt he felt while exiled from his homeland. The God who intercepted Paul on the road to Damascus is the God who intersects our lives whenever and wherever we are going.

God creates. God delivers. God feeds. God heals. God rescues. God suffers. God welcomes. God judges. God loves. God saves. That is what God does. It is all there in almost every section of the Bible. Without question, the clearest revelation of God comes in the person of Jesus Christ. However, the contents of the Bible also illuminate our understanding of God. Consider only a minimal accounting of what the biblical revelation tells us about God that profoundly affects us as persons.

God is love. The author of the little epistle of 1 John declared definitively, "God is love" (4:8). His statement was not a projection of personal aspiration or the wish of a lofty imagination but rather a succinct summary of the whole sweep of biblical revelation. God disclosed the love at the center of the divine nature in both creation and redemption.

Innumerable episodes of revelation erased all questions about the loving nature of the sovereign God. A patient, creative, forgiving love pervaded God's covenant relationship with the people of Israel. Hosea's foolish love for his wayward wife, Gomer, and redemptive action in response to her betrayal of that love provided a vivid picture of the extent to which God's love goes in caring for humankind. Later, Jesus embodied the love of the God he incarnated. Subsequently, disciples of Jesus committed themselves to live by love as a direct response to God's love, to the God who is love.

God opposes oppression. At least from the moment God, through Moses, instructed the pharaoh of Egypt to release the Israelites from slavery (Exodus 3–4), many people understood God's opposition to oppression, favor for the oppressed, and passion for liberation. Compassion and consistency mark the record of God's involvement in liberation. God identified with the poor and mistreated in society, those outcast because of disease or immorality, and individuals burdened by religion. Through prophets, historians, and evangelists, God called for justice, sharing, mercy, and liberation. More importantly, God took on the identity of deliverer or liberator.

A word picture from the Old Testament conveys an interesting insight. The root word for *salvation* means "plenty of space." Attending to the imagery of this term, we see that God saves people by setting them in a large space so they cannot be hemmed in by evil. God opposes slavery to sin, bondage to governments, and every other kind of oppression. All who recognize God as the author of salvation need to understand that, for God, salvation and liberation go hand in hand.

Jesus assumed the mantle of liberator, blessing the poor, healing the sick, giving sight to the blind and mobility to the lame, challenging social prejudices, and forgiving sins. Note the centrality of freedom in Jesus' announced agenda for his public ministry:

"The Spirit of the Lord is upon me,
because he has anointed me to preach good news to the poor.
He has sent me to proclaim release to the captives
and recovering of sight to the blind,
to set at liberty those who are oppressed,
to proclaim the acceptable year of the Lord."
                                                —Luke 4:18-19

Not without intention, Luke chose the Greek word for *exodus* to describe Jesus' departure or death (9:31). John praised Jesus as the liberator—"If the Son makes you free, you will be free indeed" (John 8:36).

Paul's understanding of God shaped him as an apostle of God's kind of freedom. The man from Tarsus challenged racial divisions and social barriers that exalted some people over others (Galatians 3:28). He critiqued the law, describing it as a helpful counselor but a destructive oppressor (Galatians 3:24-25). On the basis of his personal experience with Christ and conscientious ministry in Christ's name, the apostle of liberty declared, "For freedom Christ has set us free; stand fast therefore, and do not submit again to a yoke of slavery" (Galatians 5:1).

God desires our good—good for all people. A ghastly idea crept into religion at some point. Folks viewed God as a deity marked by anger and moved by an appetite for appeasement. If not pampered, begged, and cajoled, this God, according to these people, either ignores individuals or inflicts them with diseases and other difficulties. Such a view of God leads to a faith filled with fear, worship laced with anxiety, and a religious life that must be carried as a heavy burden. But the Bible reveals God as one who desires good for all people. Indeed, the whole of the scriptural story—from creation through redemption to the anticipated consummation—accounts for God's plenteous provisions for the benefit of all of the highest order of creation.

God gave people freedom and a will to use it. When people abused their liberty and frustrated the purpose of God, rather than give up on people, God worked to restore the primacy of good. God gave laws as a sign of continuing love. Commandments from God represent God's effort to guide us into lives of dignity and integrity. God's laws aim not at restricting life or depriving anyone of anything good but at moving life toward a fulfillment marked by peace and joy. Deuteronomy 5:29 conveys the intention of God, "If only they would always honor me and obey all my commandments, so that everything would go well with them and their descendants forever" (GNB). God wants the very best for people, for us.

Jesus, the ultimate revelation of God, embodied God's will for good for everybody. "I have come in order that you might have life—life in all its fullness," Jesus said (John 10:10, GNB). An early follower of Jesus stated this essential truth in a little different manner: "God . . . wants everyone to be saved and to come to know the truth" (1 Timothy 2:3-4, GNB).

Consider God's most-prized values in interpersonal relationships. God insists that we treat each other at least with justice, all the while nudging us toward faith bent on practicing mercy. At the center of revealed religion, God placed compassion for persons in need, identifying acts of helpfulness with the essence of righteousness. God wants care for all people. Thus, biblical revelation leads to a solid conclusion. God wills life and health, freedom and food, joy and peace, salvation and purpose, for every person. God is our friend, not our enemy. God wills our good. God wills good for everybody.

God keeps promises. The preaching of the early church— the *kerygma*—developed around a recurring outline of emphases (see Acts 1–10 for speeches attributed to Peter and Romans 1:16-32; 5:1-11; 1 Corinthians 11:23-32; 15:3-11; and Philippians 2:6-11 for some of the speeches attributed to Paul). The first of the four points in this kerygmatic outline identifies God as a keeper of promises. (Points two through four of the kerygma proclaim the appearance of the Messiah; the identification of the Messiah as Jesus who was crucified, raised from the dead on the third day, and exalted to God's right hand; and the necessity of every person repenting, believing, being baptized, and receiving the Holy Spirit.)

Peter described the Pentecost event in Jerusalem as God's fulfillment of an ancient promise heralded by the prophet Joel (Acts 2:16). After reviewing God's dealings with Abraham,

Joseph, and other patriarchs, Stephen summoned his listeners to the God whose present actions represented the fruition of that "time of the promise" (Acts 7:17). The apostle Paul referred to Jesus as the "Yes" to all God's promises (2 Corinthians 1:19-20).

Paul's declaration represented a radically new element in the realm of religion. Only in Christianity does one find the claim that all the promises of God are realized in a single person. The truth is sweeping and compelling—the God who engendered hope through numerous promises in the past aggressively worked in history to assure the realization of all that has been promised. (The verb tenses in this statement can be changed, and the truth is left unaltered—God engenders hope through promises that God works aggressively to keep.) We can count on what God says—no exceptions. God keeps all the promises God makes. Think of the confidence for living inspired by knowing God's promise-keeping nature.

"I am the LORD your God" (Exodus 20:2). These words of grace and promise that introduce the Ten Commandments echo God's statement to Abraham—"I will establish my covenant . . . to be God to you" (Genesis 17:7)—which reverberates through all of Scripture. God has taken the initiative to establish a relationship with us. A relationship with God is ours for the accepting. The only reason anyone fails to experience a life of fellowship with God is a personal choice to say no to God's welcoming love.

"God will supply every need of yours according to his riches in glory in Christ Jesus" (Philippians 4:19). Note carefully the scope of this wonderful promise. God holds out no hope for the fulfillment of all our wishes or the satisfaction of all our desires. This assurance of divine provision addresses our basic needs, which remain a part of our lives even though we enjoy a relationship with God. Within that relationship, though, we realize resources from God that enable us to deal with our needs. In the process, we see our faith enriched and our hope encouraged. Living in fellowship with God, we often discover light in the midst of dark times and strength welling up out of weakness.

"My grace is sufficient for you, for my power is made perfect in weakness" (2 Corinthians 12:9). The apostle Paul's personal experience provides a precedent that informs our expectations regarding God's provisions in times of trouble. God does not remove problems from our lives so much as offers us a way through the problems we face—note "Though I walk *through* the valley of the shadow of death, . . . thou art with me" (Psalm 23:4, emphasis added). On three occasions, the great missionary from Tarsus prayed for the removal of a serious malady in his life. However, Paul learned of God's faithfulness, not in an escape from his difficulty but in a grace that allowed him to live victoriously despite his difficulty. The assurance of God's unmerited goodness fills us with confidence regardless of the difficulties around us or within us.

"I will be with you always" (Matthew 28:20, GNB). Among the last words of Jesus' public ministry as described in the Gospels emerges this profoundly comforting comment. Its implications are staggering. We never have to be alone—never. No experience of life takes us beyond God's love or outside God's care. God's presence accompanies us through all our days and welcomes us into a new realm of reality once our days on earth come to an end.

The Bible illumines our understanding of the nature of God. What we learn about God from the Bible's recounting of the mighty acts of God throughout history evokes love and commitment in relation to God, compassion and service in relation to other people, and faith and hope for all our days.

A Book of Convictions

The Bible supplies the convictions needed to construct a solid foundation for personal thoughts and actions. My friend Wayne Oates likens convictions to the spinal column in the body. Convictions constitute the foundation of our lives—giving us support and enabling us to move but refusing to bend beyond certain points. Convictions supply us with commitments and make possible both the stability and flexibility, the certainty and integrity, so essential in a good life. From well-thought-out convictions come priorities, goals, and values that inform sound decision making and guide responsible actions. In every person's life, strong convictions are to spiritual maturity what a strong spinal column is to physical mobility.[1]

But where does one get such convictions? Frankly, a crowded marketplace of sources surrounds us—culture, family, media, peers—the list is virtually endless. However, the Bible knows no equal as a collection of convictions upon which and around which to build a meaningful and purposeful life. Consider a few biblical truths that, if embraced as personal convictions, inform and enhance every aspect of our lives.

We are people of infinite worth made in God's image. The author of Genesis tells us that we are made in the image of God. New Testament writers agree that God loves all of us and that Jesus died so all can be redeemed. What powerful commentary on the inestimable value that resides within every individual! No one created and loved by God can be judged unimportant. No one for whom Jesus died can be considered worthless.

One day years ago Howard Thurman took his two young daughters for a walk in a southern city. When the little girls ran over to a swing set on a public playground, Thurman had to explain to them sad circumstances that prevented people of color from using those swings. With his characteristic genius, Thurman told his daughters that it required the state legislature, courts, sheriffs, white churches, mayors, banks, businesses, and a majority of white people in the state to keep them from playing on those swings. "That is how important you are!" Thurman told his daughters, "You are two very important little girls. Your presence can threaten the entire state of Florida." The serenity, wisdom, courage, and confidence of Howard Thurman in a troublesome situation can be traced to his unwavering conviction about personal worth shaped by biblical truth.

Understanding ourselves as people of value created in the image of God delivers us from the perils of both conceit at one extreme and low self-esteem at the other. Though made in the image of God, we are not gods, totally self-sufficient individuals who can master all things. We have no reason to be conceited. Yet, we represent the highest order of God's creation and live

---

1. Wayne E. Oates, *Convictions That Give You Confidence* (Philadelphia: Westminster, 1984), 26.

as recipients of God's love and grace. We have every reason to feel important. Our worth defies measure. Our potential transcends limits.

A principle called *personalism* grows out of the biblical affirmation of personal worth and stands as a guide for both decision making and action. Simply stated, people are forever more important than things—than institutions, plans, profits, and the like. No individual represents an exception to that rule. People who possess this biblically informed conviction counter all forces of depersonalization with impassioned resistance and sustained enthusiasm.

We find life's greatest meaning in a relationship with Jesus Christ. All of us are capable of incredible good and despicable evil. Few of us realize the moral heights we can reach or the moral depravity to which we can sink. This much is sure though: if we must depend upon our achievements alone to guarantee a true experience of the goodness of life, we are sunk. A realization of the security and abundance that God intends for our lives develops only as we devote ourselves to living as disciples of Jesus Christ.

Jesus defined the motivation of the Incarnation as a life-giving endeavor—"I came that they may have life, and have it abundantly" (John 10:10). Not surprisingly, then, Jesus delivers us from the need to measure the quality of our lives on the basis of our moral achievements or failures by ushering us into a realm ruled by God's grace. Jesus enables his disciples to live fully human lives, experiencing freedom and finding joy in the service of love.

We never find fulfillment and happiness as the result of a search. Each is a derivative quality of life, not an end in itself. Neither can be realized in isolation from something else. Pursuits of joy usually end in misery; quests for fulfillment slide into profound disappointment. Meaning, fulfillment, happiness, and joy develop when building loving relationships and serving people in need—the very involvements so integral to a life centered on following Christ.

Authentic faith finds social expression. Faith is a very personal matter. One individual cannot resolve the issue of commitment to Christ or devotion to God for another individual.

Christ's call to discipleship requires a personal response. At the same time, personal faith is far from a private matter. A true commitment to Christ propels the committed one into redemptive actions among people in need and prompts responsible behavior in all aspects of society.

The structure of Scripture as well as words of Scripture underscore the social relevance of personal faith. In the pivotal summation of people's basic religious duties revealed on Mount Sinai, devotion to God results in compassionate behavior among neighbors. Following the first four commandments in the Decalogue, which focus on rightly relating to God, come six commandments outlining proper relationships with other people. True to this pattern of instruction, the great prophets of Israel linked their call for people to worship God with a commission imploring people to serve their neighbors in need. In this same tradition, Jesus wed love for God with service to others. Then, he modeled what he taught.

Most of Paul's letters to the early Christians exhibit the basic combination of personal faith and social ministry. Virtually every piece of the apostle's correspondence can be divided into a section on the theology of personal faith and a section on the morality of social ministry. Paul's letter to Christians in Rome exemplifies this pattern. A profound elaboration of personal faith fills the first section of Romans (twelve chapters in our Bible). Then, with the powerful transitional word "therefore," Paul turned his attention to a faith-full person's responsibilities related to other people. He discussed the role of Christians in government and the proper posture of Christians toward the weakest members of society.

The little book of James in the New Testament presents a remarkable summation of the teachings of Jesus. The author of this brief epistle so tightly wove together material on personal faith and admonitions regarding responsible social behavior that the fabric of his witness appears seamless. One bold comment in James stills all debate about the relationship between faith and action: "Religion that is pure and undefiled before God and the Father is this: to visit orphans and widows in their affliction, and to keep oneself unstained from the world" (1:27).

The greatest acts of Christian devotion involve helpfulness to people who are hurting or in need.

Christ commissions us and other people like us to be the church. Jesus entrusted his mission—the message and ministry of redemption—to his followers known as the *ekklesia*, the "called-out ones," the church. Cognizant of Jesus' commission, Paul counseled believers to consider themselves "stewards of the mysteries of God" (1 Corinthians 4:1), that is, managers or administers of the gospel. Christian fellowships function as the contemporary body of Christ, extending the ministry of Jesus—preaching, teaching, healing, and reconciling—into the world today.

Frankly, God's plan for the church may strike us as a serious mistake, at least at first glance. Contemplating the magnitude of the holy task entrusted to the church, we see ourselves as too weak, too flawed, to accomplish God's purposes. That feeling is not new. After the Resurrection, when Jesus outlined the worldwide mission entrusted to his disciples, only eleven, not twelve, stood before him. One disciple had failed miserably and left the fellowship. Even among the eleven who remained, one had denied Jesus vociferously, two had locked themselves into a struggle for power, others had demonstrated a total lack of spiritual understanding, and all—*all*—of the eleven had deserted Jesus at the time of his crucifixion. Could any group of people seem less suitable, more unpromising, for the missionary task?

The treasure of the gospel resides in "earthen vessels," as Paul observed (2 Corinthians 4:7). God does holy work through less-than-holy people, through individuals marked by all the flaws of fragile clay pots. Divine strength flows into human weakness. The whole history of redemption abounds with episodes in which God brings good out of bad situations. Jesus knew what he was doing, commissioning people like us to be the church—the teary-eyed disillusioned and the wide-eyed faithful, the angered or disappointed individual who has made a bad mistake and the hopeful or optimistic person who has enjoyed a grand success. The power of the gospel pervades our fellowship. God can and does work through all of us.

God calls us. In his helpful work on convictions, Wayne
Oates found that a person's commitment to a sense of calling
(vocation, responsibility, or life task) transcends all other
convictions as a source of courage, enthusiasm, and produc-
tivity. Undergirding the many facets of truth that the Bible
commends as candidates for personal convictions, the Bible
conveys God's call for personal commitment to a life of service. Obedience to this divine summons shapes an individual's
identity and provides a durable conviction that instills confidence, nurtures faith, and sustains energy. God calls all of us.
God calls each of us.

A Book of Direction

The Bible offers moral and spiritual direction for our lives.
The Bible is a book of faith—written *from* faith *to* faith *for*
faith—not an ethical-code book or a manual for behavior to be
consulted prior to every act or decision in the course of a day.
The Bible does not offer an answer to every question regarding
spirituality or prescribe a resolution for every moral dilemma.
Many major aspects of contemporary life are not specifically
addressed in the Scriptures. Yet, the Bible offers guidance and
counsel of inestimable worth for every person's life.

Consider a few representative scriptural admonitions, ad-
herence to which carries profound consequences for a meaningful life. Keep in mind that all such biblical counsel represents
more than the wisdom of the ages. In each instance, it is the
word of God.

Praise God. One of the most persistent pieces of counsel in
the Bible stresses the importance of offering praise to God. This
activity belongs at the center of both individuals' lives and
congregational worship.

Calls to praise resound throughout the Hebrew hymnal in the
Old Testament (for example, Psalms 111:1; 112:1; 113:1; 117:1).
The Psalms abound as well with words and phrases useful in
the execution of praise—"Thou, O LORD, art a shield about me,
my glory, and the lifter of my head" (Psalm 3:3); "O LORD, our
Lord, how majestic is thy name in all the earth!" (8:1); "I love
thee, O LORD, my strength" (18:1); "Great is the LORD and greatly

to be praised" (48:1); "Blessed be the LORD, the God of Israel, from everlasting to everlasting!" (106:48).

Why is the praise of God so important? The author of Psalm 106 cited one reason—God's "steadfast love endures for ever" (v. 1). There are more. God merits praise because of who God is and what God does. However, the biblical directive to praise God stems from our identity as persons as well as from God's divine nature. In the praise of God, we most profoundly express who we are and move toward our fullest potential as God's people. Losing ourselves in praise, we find ourselves as persons. The old Westminster Catechism stated the truth most clearly, asserting that the chief end of every individual is to praise God and enjoy God forever.

"He has shown you . . . what is good" (Micah 6:8). In this remarkable passage in the Old Testament book of Micah, the prophet summarized God's expectations for a person. His succinct summary provides fundamental instruction on how to live.

Like other biblical texts of this genre, Micah described religion relationally. God derives more pleasure from right relationships than from material sacrifices and cultic rituals. Good religion consists of horizontal and vertical dimensions—two parts horizontal to one part vertical according to Micah. Walking humbly with God involves working for justice in society and practicing loving-kindness among all people. The Decalogue also considered a healthy relationship with God inseparable from responsible social relationships. Much later a New Testament writer explained the principle at stake here: people who do not love their brothers and sisters—images of God—whom they can see are not likely to love God whom they cannot see (1 John 4:20).

Good religion is both moral and practical. At a minimum, it consists of justice, loving-kindness, and humility. *Justice* describes a basic respect (attitude) for other people's rights and efforts (action) to establish and preserve communal well-being. *Mercy* is another name for *loving-kindness* (the Hebrew word is often translated "steadfast love"). Practicing mercy requires emulating God's disposition and actions toward us— taking the initiative for good among people who do not deserve it. *Humility* is the opposite of arrogance, a quiet and patient waiting before God filled with eagerness to hear God's Word and to do God's will.

Micah's divinely inspired counsel occurred in a context that highlighted the importance of its specifics with an implied admonition: nothing is more needed than this kind of religion. Obviously, the context in which we read Micah's words differs from the setting in which he wrote them. However, the prophet's definition of healthy religion and admonition regarding its importance remain intact.

Judge not. A major theme in the teachings of Jesus (Matthew 7:1), not surprisingly echoed throughout the New Testament (Colossians 2:16; James 4:11), prohibits us from passing judgment on each other. The exercise of moral discretion is not in question, for responsible persons exercise discernment regarding various types of behavior. Yet making good decisions about one's own life differs significantly from pronouncing judgment on another person's life. Everyone is to do the former; no one is to do the latter.

No person possesses enough expertise or knowledge to judge another person. At best, our attempts at passing judgment on others rest on outward appearances and subjective hunches. Only God knows people's motives as well as actions, reality rather than perception. God alone possesses the competence to judge people. Heeding Jesus' warning against judging saves us from a lot of trouble. When one person judges another, everybody ends up getting hurt—the self-appointed judge as well as the judged. Directing judgment at another person requires playing God—a most dangerous game.

Self-interest, if not a concern for obedience, should encourage compliance with this counsel from Jesus. According to Jesus, people who persist in withholding grace in relation to others and insist upon responding to them with judgment thereby establish the basis on which God will relate to them (Luke 6:37) and the criteria by which God will judge them. What a terrifying thought! How much better life goes when we reach out to each other with reconciling grace rather than with divisive judgment.

Love one another. Admonitions to live in love pervade the Bible. In a statement that shocked his contemporaries (Mark

12:29-31), Jesus joined the ancient commandment to love God (Deuteronomy 6:5) with the mandate that called for neighbor love patterned after self-love (Leviticus 19:18). His point could hardly be missed—devotion to God leads to a desire for the well-being of your neighbor. If you love God, you will love your neighbor. That was not Jesus' last word on the subject. Late in his ministry, Jesus moved beyond the greatest of the Old Testament laws and instructed his disciples, "Love one another; even as I have loved you" (John 13:34). Jesus removed from loving relationships all concerns about rights, privileges, and merits, so much a part of self-love, and directed his followers to relate to other persons with self-giving love and grace.

Reflections on practical implications of Jesus' love admonition fill the New Testament. Loving other people means, at the very least, extending hospitality and contributing to the fulfillment of individuals' needs (Romans 12:9-13), speaking truthfully (Ephesians 4:15), demonstrating gentleness and humility (Ephesians 4:2), responding to evil with good (Romans 12:21), and offering service apart from a spirit of fear (Galatians 5:6; 1 John 4:18). Love for others does not require a reciprocal response of love. Anyone can be good to someone who is liked. Jesus challenged his disciples to demonstrate love for their enemies and to pray for people who did them wrong (Matthew 5:44). The greatest demonstration of love emulates the self-giving love of Jesus—laying down life for a friend (John 15:13).

An old story, probably apocryphal, recalls John's last sermon before a congregation. The elderly disciple only said, "Little children, love one another." He repeated the phrase over and over. Many in the audience thought John's senility had taken a toll on his oratory. In reality, the faithful man's words accurately summarized the teachings of Jesus and commended an instruction at the heart of the gospel.

A Book of Inspiration

The Bible inspires us, encouraging our relationship with God, nurturing our spirituality, and motivating us in ministry. Bible translation organizations like the American Bible Society and Bible distribution organizations like the Gideons strive to make copies of the Bible accessible to as many people as possible. On several occasions, a friend of mine has risked serious legal repercussions to smuggle Bibles into countries that officially prohibited importation of them. Why? Obviously, the mind-set behind these missions reflects great confidence in the Bible's ability to inspire its readers. A passion for making the Bible available to all people grows out of a conviction that the Scriptures minister to receptive persons—inspiring continued study, interest in salvation, openness to an encounter with Christ, and a will to order life out of devotion to God.

The Bible's ability to inspire its readers should come as no surprise to anyone familiar with the Scriptures. That particular ministry of the Scriptures appears within the Scriptures themselves. Many New Testament personalities cited, if not directly quoted, passages from the Hebrew Scriptures that inspired them. In his ministry of preparation for the advent of the Messiah, John the Baptist turned to the scroll of Isaiah (40:3-5) for words of inspiration, direction, and proclamation (Matthew 3:3). Jesus drew inspiration from the Hebrew Scriptures at several crucial points in his life: using truths from Deuteronomy 6:13, 16 and 8:3 to resist temptation; embracing a vision from Isaiah (61:1-2) to set forth the agenda for his public ministry; relying on prophetic oracles (Isaiah 56:7; Jeremiah 7:11) to define the nature of a true place of worship; and turning to the hymn text of Psalm 22 to find sustaining strength during his redemptive dying. Philip found the Old Testament a helpful source of inspiration for speaking about Jesus (Acts 8:32-33; compare Isaiah 53:7-8). Peter turned to the ancient prophecy of Joel to comment on the dramatic appearance of God's Holy Spirit (Acts 2:16-21; compare Joel 2:28-32).

Hounded by threats of persecution, early Christians found much-needed inspiration for perseverance in the Hebrew Scriptures. Psalm 34:10-16 helped them keep in focus the nature of their calling and blessing (1 Peter 3:10-12). Proverbs 11:31 encouraged suffering in accordance with God's will (1 Peter 4:18). Throughout the book of Revelation, Old Testament texts provided strength and encouragement for people of faith caught in difficult circumstances. What worked back there and then works here and now as well. At the center of the book of

Revelation (11:15) appears a source of inspiration from which I have drawn repeatedly during difficult times in my life: "The kingdom of the world has become the kingdom of our Lord and of his Christ, and he shall reign for ever and ever." I know of no promise more inspiring to a person struggling with a sense of doubt or defeat. The difficulty of the moment remains, but certainty about the future inspires durable hope.

The apostle Paul expressed great confidence in the Scriptures' ability to inspire people to develop faith and live faithfully. Inspired himself by Isaiah 52:7, Paul emphasized the importance of speaking the good news about Christ to inspire others: "How can they believe in One about whom they have not heard? . . . Faith comes from hearing what is told, and hearing through the message about Christ" (Romans 10:14, 17, Williams translation). Those of us who have watched winds of freedom sweep across the world have noted firsthand the power of the Bible to inspire life-transforming actions. In our own land, we saw the civil rights movement feed off the inspiration of the Bible in challenging prejudice, confronting unjust laws, and courageously working for social justice. Much of the heroism in that history-altering movement defies explanation apart from the inspiration of the Scriptures.

During Andrew Young's tenure as the United States' ambassador to the United Nations, he traveled extensively in the developing nations of Africa. Following a visit to that region of the world in which he enjoyed numerous contacts with common citizens as well as government officials, Young reflected on the enthusiasm for freedom he witnessed. Ambassador Young explained that the leadership responsible for the liberation movements and the emergence of new nations all over Africa learned they were free when somebody put a New Testament in their hands and told them they were God's children. Young dubbed the biblical material on freedom "very potent stuff." Potent indeed! The Bible is a book of powerful inspiration.

A Sacramental Book

The Bible transforms our lives, making present its truths and fulfilling its promises. Theologians define a *sacrament* as a visible sign of invisible grace. More simply stated, the word *sacrament* identifies any medium of grace, anything that enables us to see and experience the transforming nature of God's initiative on behalf of our good. My Baptist denominational family has traditionally shied away from the word *sacrament*, fearing it endows the ordinary with too much holiness or subtly suggests a form of magic. Christians in other traditions, however, readily describe baptism and Communion as sacraments. Still others assign a sacramental status to acts of worship such as penance and confirmation.

I see the Bible as a sacramental book. That means I experience the Bible as a collection of literature in and through which God confronts me (us) with the blessing and responsibilities of grace. The Bible ushers into the present moment the very reality it describes in its recollections of the past. Far more than a commendation or description of truths to be studied, the Bible engages us with truth.

The Bible introduces us to the concept of grace, but there is more. While reading the Bible, we encounter grace, realize relief from burdensome guilt, and experience forgiveness. Grace courses through the veins of our spiritual lives. Similarly, the Bible instills hope within us as well as identifies hope for us and commends hope to us. Scriptural narratives that document how our predecessors found hope in densely dark moments of the past incite light-giving hope within us for the present.

Not only does the Bible call us to faith; passage after passage in the Bible introduces us to faith, elicits the birth of faith within us, encourages and strengthens the faith we already hold, and further shapes us as people of faith. The Holy Book, which exalts love, fills us with love. The very Scriptures that mandate that we love one another equip us to obey that command. The Bible moves us to live by love.

The real promise of the Bible resides in its ability to bring about the changes in life for which it calls. Time and time again it happens. While reading the Bible, grieving people sense comfort, depressed people realize encouragement, anxious people know calm, fearful people find reassurance, people plagued by tentativeness discover certainty. Please, do not ask me how it happens. I can neither define nor explain the mystery and potency of the Bible's ministry. I simply recognize God working through the book we call the Word of God.

Aleksandr Solzhenitsyn witnessed the power of the Bible's ministry in the face of forbidding circumstances. While imprisoned amid terrible conditions, Solzhenitsyn noticed the serene spirit and cheerful attitude of a man who occupied the bunk above his own. Closely watching this man in an attempt to discover some reason for his good nature, Solzhenitsyn observed that each evening after retiring to his bunk, the fellow pulled from his pocket small pieces of paper and read words that had been scribbled on them. Later the famous Russian author discovered that the words on the man's papers had been copied from the Bible, from the Gospels specifically. Solzhenitsyn marveled at how, in a grisly situation, biblical words barely legible on small scraps of paper transformed their reader from a broken and bitter prisoner into a loving human being.

Perhaps the most important aspect of reading the Bible regularly involves not our application of its texts to contemporary situations but our experience of its God-given power to transform our lives. The Bible enables us to live in the very manner in which writer after writer in the Bible declares we should live. The provisions of the Bible bring to fulfillment the promises of the Bible—a complete person devoted to God whose faith in Christ finds redemptive expression in service to other persons. If dealing with the Bible is in any sense a bother—a bother like breathing, eating food when hungry, or drinking water to quench a raging thirst—the testimony of the Scriptures, the evidence of history, and convictions born of personal experiences combine to form the strong confession, "It is worth the bother!"

CHAPTER 2

For God's Sake, Be Honest

Much of what I learned about the Bible, I learned the hard way. For years, I struggled with flawed information about the Bible that made my study of the Bible difficult. Finally, people I trusted challenged me to undergo the discomfort of changing my mind. At that point, prior assumptions had to be corrected, misunderstandings revised, and new methods of study developed—no easy task once habits have persisted for a while. In retrospect, I wish someone had given me a more honest, as well as a more comprehensive, introduction to the Bible much earlier in my life.

It is one thing to say the Bible is the Word of God, but quite another to define what that means. How and when is the Bible the Word of God? Is all of it—every personal word, popular parable, cultural norm, national tale, and social tradition in the Bible—the Word of God? How do you know? Coming to grips with basic truths about the Bible up front helps us avoid erroneous approaches to Bible study and enhances encounters with the Bible that result in engagements with the Word of God. Let me be specific. Here are a few fundamental truths about the Bible. Wishing I had known these truths earlier in life, I eagerly share them with you.

The word *holy* describes the content of the Bible, not the physical book that conveys it.

During childhood, a church friend reprimanded me for underlining a verse in the Bible I carried to Sunday school each week. This well-intentioned playmate explained that we should not make marks on the pages of a Bible because the Bible is a holy book. Similarly, I heard neighboring parents scold one of their children for placing a magazine on top of a Bible that lay on a coffee table in their living room. "Nothing should ever be placed on top of the Bible," the mother warned her young child. "That shows disrespect for the Bible as a holy book."

True, the Bible is a holy book that merits respect, attention, and obedience. However, it is not a book to be worshiped. That would be idolatry (bibliolatry). The Bible conveys the Word of God, but the Bible is not equal to God. It is neither eternal nor perfect. So, in what sense is the Bible holy? Are the cover, binding glue or threads, and pages of a Bible holy? Or does the holiness of a Bible reside in its content—the spiritual message of a Bible not the physical medium in which it is presented?

Without question, early Christians considered the Hebrew Scriptures holy—Holy Scriptures. They attached ascriptions such as "God said," "Thus says the Lord," or "the Holy Spirit spoke" to quotations from the Old Testament (see Acts 1:16 and 2 Corinthians 6:16 for examples). God's people equated such scriptural declarations with the Word of God. Progression marked their thoughts—God is holy, so the Scriptures that convey God's Word are holy.

Actually, interest in the holiness of the Bible grows out of concern about the authority of the Bible. To call the Bible holy is to recognize and affirm the Bible's authority. This very assertion, though, prompts more questions. What is the source of the Bible's authority? Should readers reverence every word in the Bible as the Word of God? Are all Scriptures equally authoritative?

The authority of the Bible resides in the source of its inspiration and in its God-given ability to lead people into salvation. Scripture writers trace the history of salvation and direct people's attention to the source of salvation. The Bible is completely reliable as a guide for people interested in the abundant life that stems from a reconciled relationship with God. Confusion about biblical authority develops when people make claims about the Bible that exceed the claims the Bible makes about itself. The Scriptures enable readers to understand God's inviting love and commend the wisdom of a person's committed response to that love. Writing about Jesus, the author of Philippians declared with unmitigated authority, "At the name of Jesus every knee should bow . . . and every tongue confess that Jesus Christ is Lord" (2:10-11). However, the Bible claims no authority in realms beyond faith and theology.

Inspiration from God did not eliminate limitations imposed upon a writer by his or her culture, education, or place in history. None of these limitations, though, compromised the authority with which these individuals wrote about God's redemptive actions. Isaiah believed in a three-storied universe (the heavens and waters above the heavens on top; the earth supported by pillars in the middle; the waters below the earth on the bottom), viewing the heavens as the throne of God and the earth as God's footstool (66:1). However, the prophet accurately understood the nature of God's mercy, conveyed comfort, and engendered hope. Paul's periodic agreement with cultural norms related to the dress of women and the grooming of men (1 Corinthians 11:2-16) did not prevent him from affirming the transcendent truth that in Christ "there is neither male nor female" (Galatians 3:28).

Sensitive readers of the Bible recognize unevenness in the authority of the Scriptures. Extended sections of the Old Testament consist of time-bound religious laws, liturgical rules, or cultic rituals of little to no importance beyond the historical period in which they were written. Clearly, not every passage in the Bible carries the same weight of insight and influence or addresses our lives with equal authority. Who would assign to the census of Levites in Numbers 3 or the list of clean and unclean animals in Leviticus 11 an importance or authority equal to that of Jesus' words about eternal life in John 3 or Paul's hymn of love in 1 Corinthians 13? The number of priestly workers in ancient Israel has no significance for me, but inspired insights into the way to experience eternal life and live in love exude crucial importance.

An affirmation of the Bible's authority comes easier than an explanation of this authority. As the Scriptures address our lives, most of us recognize a power of relevance and guidance that we simply cannot translate into words. A certain degree of indefinability about the Bible's authority prevails. I find great affinity with Reformation writers who acknowledged the self-evident holiness and authority of the Scriptures. A desire to understand the authority of the Bible requires reading and studying the Bible. No one can satisfactorily describe what another can actually experience in a personal encounter with the Bible. Not infrequently when we study a passage of Scripture, the power and authority of truth touch the heart of our spirituality and evoke an "Amen." What we readily recognize as reality, we are powerless to explain. Through the words of persons in another time and place, the Word of God addresses us with self-evident authority.

I still embrace the affirmation that, as a child, I learned to sing in the booster choir of my home church, "Holy Bible . . . precious treasure, thou art mine, mine to tell me whence I came, mine to tell me who I am."

The Bible is a human book and a divine book.

In the Bible, as in the church, God chose to work through imperfect individuals. As the apostle Paul observed, earthen vessels transport divine truth into our midst (2 Corinthians 4:7). The humanity of the writers of Scripture cannot be denied. Neither can the divinity of the message they bring us.

A Human Book

Each contributor to the Bible wrote out of a particular educational background, influenced by individual biases, skilled in a unique literary style, and committed to a very personal faith. Diversity among the writers is obvious to almost every reader. So, too, is an amazing unity in their message.

A careful reading of the Bible yields insights into ideological characteristics peculiar to individual authors. A powerful nationalistic prejudice pervades the narratives of the Old Testament's Deuteronomic historian. Recurring concerns for women and the poor mark the gospel message of Luke. Mark betrays an at times almost humorous impatience with the disciples of Jesus. Convictions about the importance of social mores surface in the letters of Paul.

Distinctive literary styles identify certain writers. Students of the Hebrew language can easily distinguish the style of Isaiah's writing from that of Jeremiah's secretary, Baruch. In the New Testament, Matthew employed a variety of Hebrew words and Old Testament images to report on the life of Jesus, while John described the Messiah drawing heavily from Greek philosophy as well as Jewish theology and couching Hebrew ideas in Greek terminology.

Sometimes witnesses of the same event reported what happened and interpreted its meaning very differently. One Old Testament historian reported that David killed a Philistine giant named Goliath, a military threat to the Jews (1 Samuel 17:1-51). Another historian cited Elhanan the Bethlehemite as the giant slayer (2 Samuel 21:19). Biblical accounts of Saul's elevation to the kingship of Israel differ on the site where the man's rise to royalty took place: Mizpah in 1 Samuel 10:17-24 and Gilgal in 1 Samuel 11:15. This same phenomenon appears in the New Testament. Matthew and Luke relate different versions of the Lord's Prayer (compare Matthew 6:9-13 and Luke 11:2-4). These same two writers also differ in their recall of the Beatitudes (compare Matthew 5:3-12 and Luke 6:20-23). Attempts to explain variations in the two accounts include suggestions that Jesus delivered the Beatitudes in two different Sermons on the Mount and offered alternative forms of the Lord's Prayer in two separate teaching sessions. Such interpretive hypotheses are unnecessary. In each instance, two people recalled the specifics of an event in a somewhat different manner. More important is the fact that the truths affirmed in the event shine through both of these later reports of it.

Variations in hearing and reporting on the same oral presentation come as no surprise. Often after I have delivered a lecture or offered a sermon, I am amazed at how differently various individuals heard and interpreted my remarks. One listener caught one emphasis while another latched on to a completely different theme. Sharing with me their reflections on my presentation, some individuals completely leave out any reference to what I considered a key thought. Similar dynamics accompanied the manner in which people listened to Jesus and later recalled what Jesus said and did. Discrepancies in how various writers heard and related to others the same event do nothing but underscore the humanity of the writers. In no way do these differences compromise the reliability of the Bible or hinder the Gospels' status as the Scripture through which Christ continues to shape his church.

The humanity of the people who wrote the Bible appears as well in the limitations of their science and world-views. Today the physical shape of the earth is certain. We have seen the beautiful sphere that is our planetary home as captured through the lens of a camera snapped in outer space. However, knowledge of the spherical shape of the earth did not develop until the fifteenth or sixteenth century. Not surprisingly, then, biblical writers described the earth as a horizontal plane, the prevailing cosmology of their time. Both Isaiah (11:12) in the Hebrew Scriptures and the author of Revelation (7:1) in the New Testament refer to the "four corners" of the earth.

Similarly, biblical authors conceived of a three-storied universe. The books of Isaiah (66:1), Genesis (28:12), Mark (1:10-11), and Acts (7:55), to name a few, describe a universe in which the earth exists underneath heaven and above a netherworld. According to this world-view, humankind inhabits the middle plain called *earth*, while God dwells in the sky above and the forces of evil roam the regions below the earth. Of course, few people embrace this three-storied view of the universe today. But, so what? Writing as products of their time who held a now outdated view of the universe in no way prohibits writers of Scripture from confronting us with enduring truths about God and challenging us to live in devotion to God.

Paul spoke for every person whose writings appear in the Bible when he confessed, "Our knowledge is imperfect and our prophecy is imperfect. . . . now we see in a mirror dimly. . . . Now

I know in part" (1 Corinthians 13:9-12). Yet, through the stumbling, stammering words of finite individuals comes the enlightening, captivating, redeeming Word of Almighty God.

A Divine Book

Once we have studied a passage in the Bible, we usually do not reflect on what Mark, Mary, or Paul said. Rather, we focus our attention on what God said. Though not every writer of Scripture prefaced each passage with "Thus says the Lord," faithful readers of the Bible know the source of the scriptural message and the audience to which it was directed. Reverence for the Bible and obedience to the Bible arise not so much because we are impressed by individual writers as because we are moved by an encounter with Almighty God.

On many occasions through the years, I have returned to Kenneth Foreman's commendation of the Bible. Without minimizing the human element so evident in the Scriptures, Foreman recognizes the divine nature of the book:

> What comes to me from the Bible . . . comes, so to speak, as though through those telephone cables which can carry many messages at the same time. I hear voices from the past, but also a message for today, every today. I hear the voices of long-dead men, but also in their voices I hear the voice of the living God. I read stories of what has happened on this earth . . . yet in these happenings I see a purpose, God's purpose, working out from generation to generation. In the Bible are words of men—what men thought, felt, believed, hoped; but in, beyond, and above these words of men, I hear the word of God.[1]

The Bible is an inspired book and an interpreted book.

Questions and explanations related to the staggering integration of divine and human elements in the Bible inevitably bring our focus to a concept of inspiration. How did various time-bound persons finite in nature come to pass along the

---

1. Kenneth J. Foreman, "What Is the Bible?" in *Introduction to the Bible*, vol. 1 of The Layman's Bible Commentary, ed. Balmer H. Kelly (Richmond: John Knox, 1959), 13.

timeless, eternal Word of God? The writer of 2 Timothy offered an explanation. He considered all Scripture "inspired by God," that is, "in-breathed" by God, to take the word literally (2 Timothy 3:16). But how did that happen? Some people argue that God moved the hand of each Scripture writer to form every word according to the divine will. Others take a less mechanical view of inspiration, though retaining the idea that every word in the Bible is precisely as God willed it. According to this point of view, the minds and hearts of Scripture writers had been taken captive by God's Spirit, who dictated every word these people wrote.

Nothing we know about God from the Bible indicates the Holy One's willingness to override the will and compromise the integrity of any person. God respects individual freedom. True to the nature revealed so clearly in the ministry of Jesus, God even respects a person's right to spurn divine love and turn down an invitation to abundant life. This God would have no part in a form of inspiration that discounted human freedom and denied personal choice. God moved in the lives of various individuals causing them to write down their varied experiences of faith. The words that appear in the Bible came from the likes of Moses, Miriam, Ezekiel, Mary, Peter, Priscilla, James, and Paul. However, the words of these various individuals contain and convey a message that came straight from God. The Bible is an inspired book.

Once the Bible went to press, the Spirit of God did not cease the work of inspiration. God moves interpreters of the Scriptures even as God moved writers of the Scriptures. Serious study of a biblical text involves sensitivity to the leadership of God, who motivated the preservation of that text. Biblical interpretation is a tricky enterprise, however. Despite our best attempts at openness to the whispers of God's Spirit, pure objectivity in Bible study is well nigh an impossibility. All of us come to the Scriptures strongly influenced by perspectives borne of our life situations. So strong are the familial and cultural forces in our lives that at times we may even confuse these external influences with the internal promptings of God.

I read the Bible as a white man who grew up in the southern region of the United States. My study of the Bible takes place amid a relatively high level of economic affluence and physical comfort in comparison with most other people in the world. Often, what I first hear from a biblical text differs dramatically from the message of that same text as discerned by a South American revolutionary who spent her childhood in the shanty of a mountaintop favella. When I read the familiar parable of the good Samaritan, for example, I usually identify with the three persons who saw a man in a ditch. Recently, however, I have met many people who read Jesus' parable from the perspective of the man who had been robbed and tossed aside to die. What a difference a point of view makes in how an individual reads and understands this intriguing tale from Jesus!

Reading transcripts of Bible-study sessions conducted in Solentiname, Nicaragua, has opened up whole new vistas on biblical truth for me.[2] Long-familiar passages of Scripture have yielded unnerving new insights—what Robert McAfee Brown called "Unexpected News"—when studied against the backdrop of a life situation different from my own.[3] Our status in life effects our interpretation of the Bible. Only with considerable discipline inspired and sustained by God can any individual rise above cultural biases and economic prejudices to hear the word of God in a passage of Scripture.

The Bible is a book of faith and a book for faith.

People of faith wrote the Bible. Though the forms of their writing varied substantially, the factor of faith in their literature remained constant. Faith in God enabled these individuals to see, hear, and feel realities missed by people devoid of such faith. Viewing history from the vantage point of faith resulted in interpretations of the causes and meanings of various events not found in accounts of these same events prepared by reporters whose work was limited to physical observations alone.

Old Testament accounts of the people of Israel escaping from slavery in Egypt via a miraculous crossing of the Red Sea differ

---

2. Ernesto Cardenal, *The Gospel in Solentiname*, 4 vols., trans. Donald D. Walsh (Maryknoll, N.Y.: Orbis Books, 1977).

3. Robert McAfee Brown, *Unexpected News: Reading the Bible with Third World Eyes* (Philadelphia: Westminster, 1984).

substantially from notations about those events recorded in the
journals of Egyptian historians. The former reflects a profound
faith in God absent in the latter. Both sets of historical narratives
are true. However, explanations behind the truths differ because
of faith. Similarly, assertions about Jesus in the Gospels of the
New Testament differ dramatically from secular estimates of
Jesus that appeared in ancient chronicles of Jewish and Roman
writers. Though Matthew identified the mother of Jesus as a
virgin named Mary, a Jewish contributor to the Talmud wrote
that Jesus was born of an adulteress. While a Roman historian
known as Pliny noted that people in Palestine worshiped a man
called Christus who was nailed to a stake, the evangelist called
John identified the crucified one as none other than the Son of
God. Faith dictated the differences in these various reports.
Authors of the Gospel literature wrote with hearts inflamed by
faith and lives dedicated to faith in Jesus the Christ.

The Bible is a book of faith, written from faith to faith for faith.
An old cliché communicates a substantial truth, "The intent of
the Bible is not to tell us how the heavens go but how to go to
heaven." The Bible is not a book of science or technology but a
book of faith. Scripture writers sought to introduce us to God,
not to impress us with their knowledge of varied subjects.

The first verse of the Bible stands as a declaration of faith
about the universe, not a scientific explanation of the universe.
How the world was created is not the subject. By whom the
world was created occupied the writer's focus. In the beginning,
God! Likewise, the last verse of the Bible declares faith. The
author of this verse was not attempting to describe how everything will end but to affirm that when everything does end, God
will remain. In the end, God!

The Bible helps us know how to live, why to live, and for what
and for whom to live. But do not look to the Bible for authoritative information on history, science, anthropology, cosmology,
and the like. Turn to the Bible for an understanding of salvation,
the authority of which is validated by personal realizations of
the abundant life promised to people of faith.

The Bible consists of many different kinds of literature, not all of which can be interpreted the same way.

Most libraries and bookstores arrange their volumes by types of literature. Separate sections house historical materials, novels, biographical works, and books of poetry on designated shelves. In many instances, individual books also carry a statement of identification—science fiction, novel, autobiography, anthology. Aware of the nature of the materials they select, readers know whether to consider the content of a particular book literally or figuratively and to read it as fact or fiction. Many different types of literature fill the vast library we call the Bible. (The word *Bible* comes from the plural form of a Greek term that means "booklets." The Bible is a library.) However, the Bible contains no differentiated sections or descriptive designations to help readers identify specific genres of literature and delineate between them. As a matter of fact, substantially different types of literature exist side by side within the Bible, often on the same page.

Different Materials

The intermingling of various literary forms within the Bible presents a major challenge to readers interested in a correct interpretation of the Bible. Failure to identify the type of material that appears in a specific Scripture passage creates a huge risk of seriously misunderstanding that part of the Bible's message. Discovering the truth in a biblical text requires an accurate identification of the nature of the literature in that block of material and employment of a method of interpretation consistent with the characteristics of that kind of literature. A brief notation of the broad categories of literature present in the Bible establishes the need for varied approaches in interpreting God's Word.

History. Many individuals wrongly consider the Bible a neat and orderly history of the people of God. To be sure, the Scriptures contain history: historical narratives that recount events, movements, deeds, and the people involved. However, not all of the Bible is history, and not all historical narratives in the Bible unfold in a neat chronological order. With few exceptions, actually, the Bible does not provide long, uninterrupted, carefully sequenced accounts of historical developments.

Most of the writers whose inspired work appears in the Bible had little interest in reporting history for the sake of history. For these people, historical developments validated the faith convictions on which they had staked their lives. They wrote history out of a concern for theology. Consequently, their writings preserve invaluable historical narratives on the one hand and present a testimony regarding God's interest and involvement in history on the other hand.

For example, take a look at 2 Samuel 12:1-7, a detailed account of a dramatic encounter between King David and a prophet named Nathan. This is good history. At the same time, this narrative provides readers with far more than historical understanding. Insights into the divine will and the nature of the moral order come from the text. Or consider the New Testament book of Acts, which abounds with historical narrative. Using this account of early Christianity attributed to Luke, readers can trace significant developments in the primitive community of faith. But there is more. Historical narratives in Acts reveal the gospel's awesome power to overcome prejudices and tear down barriers in its expansive ministry.

Prophecy. Prophetic literature dominates the Old Testament. Much, if not most, of this material first existed as spoken words—oracles, declarations, sermons. Only later did a secretary to a prophet or a follower of a particular prophet write down what that spokesman from God had said. For this reason, many passages of prophecy can be better understood when heard than when read.

Prophets labored to make people listen to them, strove to lodge their messages in a community's memory. Toward that end, they often combined prose and poetry as well as employed unforgettable puns, figures of speech, and plays on words. Prophetic speech achieved extensive influence through the use of powerful terminology—words that impressed, incited, and overwhelmed listeners—rather than by tightly structured, carefully reasoned forms of persuasion. Prophetic attacks on immorality made people feel the danger of evil, not just think about it.

Liturgy. Materials regularly used in the worship experiences of Israel and the early church both influenced the development of the Scriptures and contributed substantially to their content. The importance of a piece of literature in people's worship practices heavily influenced decisions about whether or not to include that piece of literature in the Bible. Thus, the Bible contains a variety of worship materials—some that instructed and guided worship and some that constituted actual words of worship.

Psalms—the songbook and prayer book of the people of God—represents the most obvious and most extensive collection of the Bible's liturgical materials but by no means all of it. Much of the book of Exodus probably first circulated as a Passover liturgy frequently used in ancient Jewish communities. Similarly, in the New Testament, the book of Revelation reflects the language of early Christian worship. The importance of the words in these materials derives not from the objective information they convey but from the faith they inspire, the visions they incite, and the praise to God they elicit.

Copies of extended prayers crop up throughout the Scriptures. Many of these prayers originally served as a single individual's offering to God in worship. Later Christian congregations incorporated these private petitions into the liturgy of their corporate worship. For example, the long personal prayer of the Old Testament prophet Habakkuk (chap. 3) became a crucial part of the early Christian church's liturgy for worship on Good Friday.

Sermons or fragments of sermons originally delivered in the context of Christian worship found a place in the Christian Scriptures. The author of Acts interspersed homiletical materials amid his historical narratives (look at Acts 3:12-26). Many scholars posit that much of the book of Hebrews first took form as a homily prepared for delivery at the baptism of new Christians.

The Bible contains a substantial number of hymns, well over seventy by most estimates, in addition to the psalms. Congregations recognize the hymnic, poetic nature of the well-known song of Hannah from 1 Samuel 2:1-10, the Magnificat (Mary's song) as found in Luke 1:46-55, and the Benedictus from Luke 1:68-79. A number of lesser-known hymns within the Bible also merit special attention and require unique interpretation—a possible baptismal hymn in Romans (13:11-14) and the great theological hymn to Christ in Philippians (2:5-11), to name but two.

A variety of other worship materials appear in the Bible. Several New Testament passages consist of confessions of faith, "Jesus Christ is Lord" (Philippians 2:11) being one of the earliest. Occasionally a unique liturgical expression shows up in a text. The author of the book of Revelation, for example, often repeated the moving exclamation of "Hallelujah" (see 19:3, 6 for the pattern), an important expression in Hebrew worship. Paul employed *Maranatha* as a benediction, the distinctive petition of Christian worshipers, which was created by a combination of two Aramaic words and translated "Our Lord, come" (1 Corinthians 16:22).

Wisdom. The Old Testament books of Proverbs and Ecclesiastes represent a type of material called wisdom literature. It appears throughout the Scriptures. In some instances, this material takes the form of short pithy sayings, brief moral maxims, fables, succinct counsel, and even riddles. More lengthy pieces of wisdom literature also exist. The book of Job is perhaps the longest as well as the grandest example of wisdom literature.

Wisdom literature contains teaching material. Some of it takes aim at correcting misunderstandings and establishing theological truth. Other pieces of wisdom material offer moral instruction. In both instances, writers intended that the substance of this literature would contribute to the maturation of personal faith and morally responsible behavior in people's lives.

Gospel. The ancient world of literature knew no precedent for the Gospel. As a unique literary form, Gospels developed to preserve the good news about Jesus and to continue his appeal for lives pervaded by grace and love and devoted to the rule of God. A Gospel unfolds the story of Jesus' life and explores the meaning of that life from the point of view of persons who believed in Jesus as the Savior of the world and confessed him as Lord. History is involved, but not all history. Even the historical narratives included in a Gospel do not trace developments in Jesus' life in a strictly chronological order.

Never intending to produce a detailed biography of Jesus (as we think of biography), each Gospel writer selected certain events, stories, miracles, and teachings from Jesus to be included in his work. Subsequently, not all the Gospels look alike. Mark's Gospel begins with the public ministry of Jesus apart from any reference to his birth, which is described briefly in Matthew and at length in Luke. The Fourth Gospel arranges events from the life of Jesus in an order that differs significantly from the sequence of his ministry presented in the first three Gospels.

A Gospel elaborates faith in a manner intended to encourage faith in all who read it. Each author of a Gospel wrote confessional theology as well as biography and history. Gospel narratives serve the purpose of gospel proclamation—"the good news."

Apocalyptic. Jewish writers developed a literary form known as apocalyptic. The Old Testament book of Daniel is a classic example of this type of literature. During the New Testament era, apocalyptic writings became extremely popular. The last book in the New Testament fits into this literary genre. Indeed, the Revelation is alternately known as the Apocalypse.

Almost invariably, apocalyptic literature emerged from times of trouble, hardship, and persecution among people of faith. Writers of apocalyptic literature believed they were living in the last days of a history preplanned by God. They supported this point of view with interpretations of history gained through special revelations and dramatic visions. In every instance, the purpose of apocalyptic writing was to encourage the people of God to remain faithful to their commitments despite adversity. Apocalyptic materials assured believers that present sufferings would be followed by salvation.

Writers of apocalyptic designated special events of the past as indicators of the world's relentless trek toward a dramatic conclusion of history already established by God. Through special interpretations of former events, apocalyptic writers calculated the exact length of time that had to elapse before present sufferings would end. Producers of this literature comfortably predicted occurrences beyond history as well as developments in history. Because apocalyptic literature arose in the face of governments and other forces hostile to Christianity, writers often conveyed their message by means of symbols, figurative language, dramatic signs, and even numbers supposedly endowed with theological meaning. Nonbelievers found confusing the very materials that brought great comfort and much-needed reassurance to believers.

Epistle. The New Testament contains numerous pieces of correspondence. Most of these letters were written by a Christian missionary and addressed to a specific congregation of believers or a specific group of Christian congregations located in a particular geographical region. Consistency in the format of these letters establishes the epistle as a distinct literary style of biblical literature.

Like most pieces of correspondence, the Letters in the New Testament focused on specific issues and situations among the persons to whom they were addressed. Consequently, counsel commended in one letter did not necessarily apply to circumstances faced by people in a different location. The letters of Paul contain material that reflects a particular time and cultural circumstance (see 1 Corinthians 11:4-12) as well as statements of faith and principles of morality (1 Corinthians 13) that are timeless in nature. A helpful interpretation of New Testament Epistles requires discernment and discretion.

Different Interpretations

We do not interpret a novel the same way we do a collection of historical essays or respond to the text of a biography as we do to a personal letter from a well-known friend. Likewise, when reading the Bible, we should not interpret a prophetic oracle and a Gospel saying or apocalyptic literature and historical narratives in the same manner.

A Gospel incorporates personal experiences, sentiments, and thoughts into a confession of faith. One person speaks to other persons about the Good News of Christ. Historical narrative tends to be less emotional and more objective than a Gospel story, focusing on factual data and reporting events more than expressing how people felt about the events. The Epistles and some pieces of wisdom literature reflect a specific time, place, culture, and religious orientation. Prophecy frequently conveys challenge, demand, and hope in flaming poetic language.

Different sources and audiences give rise to different kinds of materials. God speaks to people through prophecy and wisdom literature. People speak to each other in narratives and Gospels. People speak to God by means of liturgy. Reactions to these literary forms vary with the interpretations appropriate for the forms. Narrative materials inform us, prophecy challenges us, wisdom instructs us, and Gospels incite faith within us. Stated another way, Gospels prompt worship, narratives prompt storytelling, prophecy leads to repentance, and wisdom results in learning.

The Bible is a creation of the church, as well as the church's critic and guide.

For a long time, I thought the Bible produced the church. Not so. Of course, the Hebrew people and the Jewish faith antedated the formation of the Old Testament. The same was true of Christian disciples and the Christian faith in relation to the New Testament. Christianity is not a religion based upon a book but a faith centered in the person of Christ. The book, the Bible as we know it, came later.

The Bible in the Church

Only over an extended period of time did the Jewish people reach any consensus about the contents of their Scriptures (the corpus of what we call the Old Testament). To be sure, as early as six hundred years before the birth of Christ, Jews considered the book of Deuteronomy as Holy Scripture (Deuteronomy was probably the "book of the law" discovered in the temple in 621 B.C. and cited in 2 Kings 22:8). Another two hundred years elapsed, however, before all of the first five books in our present Old Testament (the Torah) were recognized as Scripture and utilized in corporate worship. The books of Psalms, Proverbs, Job, Song of Solomon, Ruth, Lamentations, Ecclesiastes, Esther,

Daniel, Ezra, Nehemiah, and 1 and 2 Chronicles were not finally added to the Hebrew Scriptures until ninety years after the birth of Christ. Similarly, agreement on what materials should be included in the New Testament did not jell quickly. Most of the present New Testament was recognized as Scripture by A.D. 170 (exceptions included the books of James, Hebrews, 2 Peter, and 3 John). However, general agreement on the New Testament as we know it today did not coalesce until A.D. 367. Even then, the church vigorously debated the inclusion of the books of James, 2 Peter, 3 John, and Jude.

Religions such as Mormonism and Islam claim that their sacred scriptures appeared intact and subsequently inspired the formation and development of their religious institutions. Not so is the claim of Christianity. Christians acknowledge that the contents of the Bible developed over a lengthy period of time. God inspired persons to write (in some instances after the materials to be written had existed in stories, sermons, and worship materials for many decades). Individuals wrote out of their own experiences of faith. Eventually the church compiled these writings. The Bible emerged from the community of faith as a witness to various expressions of that faith.

A recognition of how the Bible developed saves us from worshiping the Bible instead of the God who inspired the Bible and revealed the divine will through the Bible. This awareness also prevents us from assigning to the Bible an authority that belongs to Christ alone.

The Bible on the Church

An interesting relationship exists between the Bible and the church. As we have seen, the Bible grew out of the life of the church. At the same time, though, the Bible critiques and counsels the community (or communities) in which it developed. A careful reading of the Bible exposes the weaknesses and growing pains of the early church. Authors of the Scriptures addressed problem areas in their communities and wrote of a better way to move toward Christian maturity.

The Bible addressed prejudice in the primitive community of faith and pushed the church to embrace a larger mission. In the book of Acts, Luke related a moving moment when Peter discovered God's intolerance of discrimination among persons of faith and heard God's mandate to move among Gentiles for fellowship (10:9-35). This same piece of New Testament literature traced the ever-expanding mission of the Christian church as it sought to comply with the commission of its Lord: "You shall be my witnesses in Jerusalem and in all Judea and Samaria and to the end of the earth" (Acts 1:8).

If you want to understand the church, read the Bible. It is the normative document for the people of God. The Bible inspires and guides the church's worship, supplying content for its liturgies, meaning for its rituals, and enlightenment for its vision. The Bible sets the agenda for the church, providing the substance for its proclamation, undergirding its teaching with wisdom, and calling forth its various ministries. The Bible nurtures the faith of church members, encouraging spiritual growth, informing ethical decision making, and counseling cooperation and unity.

One interpretation of a biblical text is not as good as another.

I once heard one of my seminary professors, for whom I had profound respect, engage a fellow church member in a discussion on a biblical text. Disagreement between the two men's understanding of the text developed quickly. After my professor explained the reasons undergirding his interpretation of the text, the other man resentfully declared, "I don't care about all your learning; I have as much right and ability to interpret this text as you do. And my interpretation is just as good as yours." I was astounded. I knew my professor's credentials in biblical languages, his experience in critical studies, and his thorough knowledge of various biblical commentaries. The other fellow's adamant comment struck me as terribly arrogant and terribly wrong.

Unfortunately, wild hunches, fly-by-night biases, and even ignorant arrogance in biblical interpretation receive credibility in some ecclesiastical circles. Well-meaning people confuse the doctrinal truth of the priesthood of every believer with a

personal ability to flaunt rank individuality in an interpretation of the Bible. I cherish the doctrine of individual priesthood among believers—the belief that every Christian is
"to relate to and act for God."[4] However, this doctrine
should not be confused with a carte blanche endorsement
of ignorance. The status of priesthood imposes a responsibility as well as bestows a blessing. A priest has an obligation
to interpret the Bible under the guidance of God's Spirit and
with a commitment to integrity, not on the basis of personal
preferences. Affirmation of the priesthood of individual interpretation fails as an endorsement for elevating personal opinion
over informed examination in relation to the Bible.

As to rights of interpretation, every individual can interpret
the Bible for himself or herself. A right to interpretation does not
guarantee a right interpretation, though. Well-intentioned interpretations of the Bible often turn out to be very wrong. However,
if the issue in question is rights, we all have the right to be
wrong. Interpreting the Scripture is never a matter of individual
opinion. Biblical interpretation begins with historical revelation
rather than personal perspective. All truth related to Scripture
results from an impulse of the Holy Spirit (2 Peter 1:20-21). God
guides the interpretation of the Bible even as God guided the
revelation that gave rise to the Bible.

The Bible is a dynamic book as well as an ancient book.

"How can a book as old as the Bible possibly have anything
important to say to people of our day?" The rather skeptical
young man who posed that question gave voice to a common
false assumption. His inquiry overlooked a basic characteristic
of the biblical revelation.

Yes, the Bible contains materials that date back hundreds of
years before the birth of Jesus. Those ancient documents clearly
reflect a cultural milieu, an understanding of history and science, religious laws, and social practices radically different from

---

4. Walter B. Shurden, *The Doctrine of the Priesthood of Believers* (Nashville:
Convention Press, 1988), 10.

all we know today. Yet, timeless words of truth resound under, in, and through those very old, time-bound materials. This ancient book makes a dynamic impact on all who engage, or become engaged by, its message. Under the inspiration of God, time-bound writers (all products of their particular period in history) passed along timeless truths of crucial importance to individuals in every age. The Bible contains much more than a message to learn, instructions to heed, or ideas to ponder. The Bible packs power. Its message enjoys a continuing ministry.

Though set in a context remote from anything current, a biblical passage can address a contemporary situation with more relevance than the morning's newspaper headlines. Moreover, the Bible helps bring about in the present the very kinds of situations from the past that it describes. It is a catalyst for positive changes, a dynamic book. The enduring truths of Scripture not only tell us something about life; they help bring about the quality of life they commend. The Bible inspires reform, engenders hope, encourages love, instills faith, causes prayer, prompts repentance, motivates ministry, does away with doubts, and prods growth.

Accessible Truth

The Bible's simplicity makes its truths accessible to almost everybody. Virtually illiterate people can discover new meaning in life as a result of Bible study. Strangely, though, the Bible's complexity confounds its most learned readers. Often the very Scripture passages that appear so simple that a child can understand them contain numerous layers of meaning and expansive circles of application that challenge the most dedicated scholars. Individuals who know the Bible best speak and write about its meaning with humility, displaying profound reverence for the depths of its mystery.

Neither highly educated people nor essentially illiterate people have any reason to boast about their approach to the Bible. One status is no more holy than the other. Regardless of the level of mental and spiritual development with which a person begins to study the Bible, the ultimate issue in that study is growth. The Bible invites both faithful study—"Do your best to present yourself to God as one approved, a workman who has no need to be ashamed, rightly handling the word of truth" (2 Timothy 2:15)—and growth—"Grow in the grace and knowledge of our Lord and Savior Jesus Christ" (2 Peter 3:18).

Writing to Christians in Corinth, the apostle Paul conveyed the spirit of Scripture study in his plea for spiritual maturation, which makes possible responsible interaction with the "meat" of the Christian faith (1 Corinthians 3:1-2). As God's people—whether uneducated or holders of advanced degrees—we are called to move from the basis of truth comprehendible at any one moment to realize the truth available to us with more growth and study under the leadership of God's Spirit.

Personally, the more informed about the Bible I have become, the more the Bible has affected my life. Learning the real nature of the Bible enhanced my appreciation for the Bible, informed my interpretation of its texts, and prodded my application of its truths to the verities of my life. My experience is not unique. Learning the Bible creates a receptivity into which God moves, enabling us to translate beliefs into behavior—what we know into how we live.

The Bible invites our toughest questions about its nature and encourages our careful scrutiny of the media of its message. As a book brimming with truth, the Bible entertains no fear of truth. When raising questions about the Bible, studying the Bible, or teaching or preaching the Bible, for God's sake—and for the benefit of all involved—be honest!

CHAPTER 3

Is There a Word from God?

King Zedekiah ruled troubled people. Enemy militia from Babylonia amassed on Judah's borders and threatened the continued existence of the nation. On several occasions, the besieged ruler sought counsel from God's prophet known as Jeremiah. In each instance, however, the political sovereign resentfully dismissed the prophet's message from God because it did not square with his own personal opinion. Completely put out with the prophet, Zedekiah eventually imprisoned Jeremiah. But that action did not halt the deteriorating situation in his nation. Finally, in the depths of a national crisis, when catastrophe appeared imminent, the king turned to the jailed prophet once more. On that occasion, Zedekiah articulated a request that reverberates through the centuries and resounds within many of our souls: Is there any word from God? (See Jeremiah 37:17.)

Spiritual sons and daughters, brothers and sisters of Zedekiah number in the millions. Far more than once, most of us have raised Zedekiah's inquiry. Trying to make sense of an apparently senseless death, a grief-stricken friend asks, "Is there any word from God?" Struggling with a complex ethical issue raised by a new procedure in the practice of medicine, a physician asks, "Is there any word from God?" Battling tough options related to a vocational move, a business associate asks, "Is there any word from God?" Trying to decide about the continuation of a marriage, a distraught couple asks, "Is there any word from God?" Attempting to handle a dreaded disease courageously, a sufferer asks, "Is there any word from God?" Negotiating contradictory pressures related to a pivotal legislative vote, a politician asks, "Is there any word from God?" Fighting depression induced by dissatisfaction with the present direction of her life, a young career woman asks, "Is there any word from God?" Mandated to make a decision or challenged to take action in a complex situation fraught with difficulties, we silently query within our minds, if not audibly ask with our voices, "Is there any word from God?"

"Yes," comes the response. A reply to our question quickly emerges from theology, history, and personal experience. Yes, there is a word from God. It may not be the word we want to hear or a word that makes our situation less difficult. But God has a word for us, for all of us.

Inquiring about a word from God causes me almost instinctively to turn to the Bible, not that the Bible is a code book, a manual of regulatory procedures, a self-help volume, or a counseling directory. It is not. However, the Bible conveys the word of God. So I take my search for a word from God to the book many people call the Word of God. I wish, however, that finding God's word for a specific situation were as easy as opening the pages of a Bible. That is not the case, though. Hearing a word from God requires discretion as well as intention, questioning as well as affirming biblical texts.

Answering Important Questions

Take a text from the Bible; any one will do. "Isn't it easy enough to know what that text means?" an individual innocently inquires. No. "But surely the truth of a passage of Scripture becomes self-evident," another protests. No, again. Interpreting the Bible correctly requires faithfully and honestly answering several important questions that relate to every biblical text. (Many of the questions treated in this chapter were first suggested to me in other forms by James Cox, who compiled them from a variety of sources, shared them with his students in preaching classes, and published commentary on them.[1]) Responding to these inquiries yields insights that prove absolutely crucial to a profitable study of Scripture. Devoid of accurate information about a specific passage in the Bible, a meaningful interpretation of that text is virtually impossible. The crucial questions follow.

What kind of literature appears in this text?

In chapter 2, I identified seven broad categories of literature that frequently appear in the Bible. Along with that enumeration, I suggested that identification of the type of literature contained in a text is crucial to a correct interpretation of that text. Now, more specifics are in order.

Within the broad classifications of literary forms contained in the Bible appear a wide variety of very particular types of literature. Each specific literary genre requires special consideration as a prerequisite for correct interpretation. Even a brief sampling of various literary forms found in the Bible alerts us to the need for flexibility and sensitivity in biblical interpretation. No singular approach to Scripture studies successfully gets at the meaning of every scriptural text.

For example, good stories fill the Scriptures. However, not all of these stories are alike. *Historical narratives* provide basic insights into nations, people, events, and life situations. *Fictional narratives* drive home important principles or truths by tying them to a memorable picture or character and illustrating them in an interesting manner. Fictional materials and historical materials obviously demand different types of interpretation.

The Gospels of the New Testament in particular contain a rich variety of story forms. *Paradigms* or *pronouncement stories* offer a brief report on an event in the life of Jesus in order to pass along an authoritative pronouncement from Jesus. The principle component in these stories is the saying to be remembered and heeded. *Miracle stories* describe Jesus as casting out demons, healing physical maladies, and exercising control over natural forces. Though these stories abound with innumerable details,

---

1. James W. Cox, *A Guide to Biblical Preaching* (Nashville: Abingdon, 1976), 49-58.

their primary purpose is not to teach lessons (as in the para-digms) but to establish the reality of Jesus' superiority. *Stories of the supernatural* strike awe and convey mystery as they report dramatic incidents in which two different worlds intersect. The Gospel account of the Transfiguration of Jesus represents this kind of story. Not uncommonly the need to explain these stories gives way to an acknowledgment of awe before the mystery they capture and convey. *Parables* weave interesting tales in order to convey important truths. No one told parables as Jesus did. Though debates continue about how best to interpret par-ables, most scholars warn against getting bogged down in the stories' details. Of primary importance is the discovery of the central truth that each story seeks to establish and preserve in a memorable manner.

Poetry appears as a popular literary form throughout the Bible. Truths conveyed by poetry are to be taken seriously, but the poetic medium resists a literal interpretation. A hymn text, for example, requires a method of understanding that differs significantly from that of a descriptive narrative.

A recurring literary device called *parallelism* often shows up in Hebrew poetry. Various types of parallelism further readers' comprehension of a major truth. In Psalm 117:1 the second line simply repeats the first line and drives home the admonition to praise God. However, in Psalm 91:1 the second line adds to a reader's understanding of the first line. In the noted confession of Psalm 51:9-12, the second line of each verse completes the truth of the statement that precedes it. Sometimes, as in Psalm 1:1-2, the author uses parallelism to draw a sharp contrast between two different situations. Within the contrast lies a crucial truth.

Intriguing instances of *picturesque language, metaphors, similes,* and other *figurative expressions* enhance the Bible's message. Jesus regularly provided insights into the nature of God's rule by likening the kingdom of God to something else—good plants and intrusive weeds growing side by side (Matthew 13:24-30), a small mustard seed that grows into a great tree (Matthew 13:31-32), leaven (Matthew 13:33), a treasure hidden in a field (Matthew 13:44), a merchant who sells all he has to buy one pearl of great value (Matthew 13:45), and a net that gathers all kinds of fish (Matthew 13:47-50). To secure an important truth in people's minds, Jesus often used *hyperbole*. No one actually expected to see a camel go through the eye of a needle, but Jesus' use of that hyperbolic image in Mark 10:25 caused people to remember forever the potential of possessions to divert people's attention from fidelity to God's rule. All of these literary devices prove extremely helpful in the cause of conveying truth. However, none of them can be pressed too tightly without losing meaning.

Distinguishing between *religious laws, civil laws, contemporary house codes (general guidelines for domestic behavior), moral maxims, proverbs,* and *catalogues of virtues and vices* is not always easy, though always necessary. The importance of a proverb drawn from culture differs significantly from that of a moral maxim taken from the teachings of Jesus. Similarly, a collection of dietary laws within the Hebrew Scriptures merits a type of attention completely unlike that devoted to Paul's summation of the "fruit of the Spirit" in a Christian's life (Galatians 5:22-23).

Commandments appear throughout the Scriptures. However, discretion regarding the nature of these mandates informs the wisest interpretation of them. According to the Gospel of John, the same night on which Jesus instructed his disciples to break bread and share a cup in his name, he also said, "You . . . ought to wash one another's feet. For I have given you an example, that you also should do as I have done to you" (John 13:14-15). Yet, most Christians consider Jesus' words about the meal, "Do this in remembrance of me" (1 Corinthians 11:24), as a mandate for repetition and interpret his exhortation about foot washing as an illustration of servanthood rather than a call to ritual. With a similar inconsistency that may serve the cause of wisdom by facilitating an accurate application, interpreters consider Jesus' command to a rich young man, "Go, sell what you have, and give to the poor" (Mark 10:21), an illustration of selfless commitment rather than a binding piece of moral legislation regarding disciples and possessions.

Written correspondence, letters from one person to another person or letters from an apostle to a specific Christian congregation or to a number of churches in the same geographical region, constitutes a large portion of the New Testament. These pieces of correspondence often address issues peculiar to a specific body of believers. Readers do well to exercise caution lest they indiscriminately try to apply advice conditioned by the dynamics of a particular situation to an altogether different context. Much of Paul's counsel to the Corinthian Christians regarding personal grooming practices and dietary habits loses its significance (and authority) for Christians in a different context.

In both the Hebrew Scriptures and the New Testament, *apocalyptic literature* requires special considerations for interpretation. Writers of this kind of material cloaked their message in symbols—symbolic images, even symbolic numbers—understandable to the faithful, but unintelligible to others. Care must be exercised lest readers confuse symbols of various realities with the realities themselves. Heeding the truth of Revelation 12:1-6, for example, involves not looking for a pregnant woman confronted by a great red dragon but recognizing the world's reaction to the advent of the Messiah. Authors of apocalyptic literature intended to encourage faith and endurance among frightened and often hurting Christians, not to sketch profiles of actual historical figures and define sequential developments in a distant future.

Is this material meant to be taken literally?

Accurately identifying the kind of literature that appears in a biblical text goes a long way to helping answer the second question to be addressed to that text. Not every verse in the Bible invites (or demands) a literal interpretation. In fact, to attempt a literal understanding of certain Scripture passages greatly obscures the meaning of those texts or altogether misses essential truths contained in them.

How do we know whether or not to take a text literally? What about a biblical passage dictates another manner of interpretation? Correct answers to these questions provide insights crucial to beneficial Bible study. Subjective hunches cannot suffice for objective standards of interpretation in mining the meaning of a text. Allow me to suggest three criteria to be considered when deciding about a literal interpretation of a passage.

First, take a close look at the context of the passage and use common sense regarding its meaning in that setting. For example, in an upper room somewhere in Jerusalem, on the night he was betrayed, Jesus offered his disciples bread and wine saying, "This is my body. . . . This is my blood" (Mark 14:22, 24). Few, if any, people believe Jesus asked his disciples to eat his flesh and drink his blood in a physical, literal sense. The context of Jesus' words—an evening meal and a discussion of Jesus' immanent passion—suggests that Jesus used a loaf of bread and a cup of wine to speak to his disciples of the impending brokenness of his body and the pouring out of his blood in the cause of redemption. The point of Jesus' words resided not in a physical consumption of flesh and blood but in the establishment of a new covenant for communion. (Interestingly, critics of the early church who overheard the words of Jesus repeated in the Communion liturgy of various congregations accused Christians of cannibalism—an accurate charge given a literal interpretation of Jesus' remarks.)

Second, decide what type of literature appears in the passage and employ a method of interpretation consistent with that literary form. Both Jesus and his prophetic predecessor Isaiah spoke of joy associated with God's deliverance. Their remarks require dramatically different methods of interpretation, though. Jesus described the consequence of salvation as abundant life, life filled with joy. He spoke matter-of-factly, and that is how his words are best understood. Isaiah used poetry to speak of God-given joy. His imagery engages the imagination rather than invites an intellectual grasp of facts:

> The mountains and the hills before you
>   shall burst into song,
>   and all the trees of the field shall clap their hands.
>   —Isaiah 55:12 (NRSV)

A literal reading of this passage in Isaiah suggests a freak of nature that distracts from the emphasis on God's liberation. A figurative understanding of the prophet's message draws readers into a cosmic celebration of the joy of God's redemption.

Third, consider the author's purpose in recording the passage. What was the author saying? Was a literal interpretation of the text suggested?

For example, apocalyptic materials fill the last book in the Bible—the Revelation. By means of symbols, signs, and numbers that non-Christians would fail to understand, the author wrote to encourage followers of Christ in a time of persecution. What a given text said paled in importance to what that text meant. Preoccupation with the images themselves, such as those associated with the vision of God in Revelation 4:1-11, can cause a reader to miss the glory of the essential truth for which the passage was written—the beauty and majesty of the God whose sovereignty is not even threatened, much less destroyed, by governmental persecution.

The author of the Fourth Gospel prepared a theological treatise on the identity, life, ministry, and meaning of Jesus. A literal reading of many of his materials presents major problems to people also familiar with accounts of Jesus' ministry in Matthew, Mark, and Luke. However, John never intended for much of his narrative to be considered literally. He was writing theology. In service to his purpose, John rearranged events, employed vivid symbols, and used figurative language. For example, John positioned Jesus' cleansing of the temple early in Jesus' ministry to demonstrate that Jesus established a new center for faith. With great artistry and skill, John offered "signs" to enhance people's understanding of Jesus—Jesus filled the ancient receptacles of religion with grand new and dynamic truths (he turned water into wine) even as he established his lordship over death as well as life (he raised Lazarus from the dead). Likewise, John reported a number of descriptive statements in which Jesus made use of figurative language—I am "the vine," "the good shepherd," "the light of the world." No serious student of the Scriptures takes these figures of speech as literal descriptions of Jesus' physical appearance.

What words or images in this passage are difficult to understand?

Answering this question correctly requires caution and sustained attention. After an initial reading of a Scripture passage, you may feel that all the words and images in it appear familiar. Beware, though. Assumed familiarity often prevents an honest grappling with a text and, thus, a thoughtful, accurate interpretation of that text.

Word meanings vary from book to book in the Bible. Different writers create new nuances of meaning for the same term. Watching for changes in the use of a word by seeking to understand its specific definition in various biblical settings is essential to a helpful interpretation of the Scriptures. History documents the importance of such cautious word study.

Covenant. For various reasons, some words in the Scriptures are difficult to understand. The term *covenant*, for instance, represents a concept that formed the core of Israel's faith in God. No one can make sense of the Old Testament apart from understanding a covenant (the term appears over 250 times in the Hebrew Scriptures). However, our society is much more prone to speak of contracts than covenants. The two are not the same. Knowing the difference between a contract and a covenant is crucial in biblical interpretation.

The Hebrew word for *covenant* (*berith*) originally meant "bond" or "fetter." People who formed a covenant forged a bond between each other (2 Samuel 5:1-3). Israel became a nation as a result of entering a covenant with God, an opportunity and a relationship made possible by God's goodness. God promised to bring blessings and salvation to Israel if Israel would respect divine authority and live according to the law revealed by God. Fidelity to the covenant meant salvation. Breaking the covenant set in motion severe consequences. The history of Israel can be told around violations and renewals of the nation's covenant with God.

Israel's hope for the future centered on the promise of a new covenant—one not based on external legal codes but on an internal spiritual relationship (Jeremiah 31:31-33). The advent of the Messiah fulfilled that hope. Jesus described his redemptive death as the event that established the new covenant: "This cup is the new covenant in my blood" (1 Corinthians 11:25). Early Christians celebrated the more excellent covenant provided by Christ (Hebrews 8:6).

Failure to understand the biblical concept of covenant can result in a radical misunderstanding of our relationship to God. Dealing with God is not like bickering with a business client over the stipulations of a contract. Contracts are legal documents that get negotiated, broken, adjudicated, and periodically rewritten. Dissimilarly, God invites us into a covenant relationship established by love and sustained by grace, a covenant without limits either in terms of time or loyalty.

The images or pictures conjured up by biblical words also play a key role in accurate scriptural interpretation. These more imaginary components of a text require the same careful study devoted to the words examined above. Look, for example, at the importance of properly understanding biblical images that inform our concept of God and our relationship to God.

Father God. References to God as "Father" cloud an accurate perception of the divine being for many individuals. Bad experiences with the father in their family blind certain persons to the positive theological truth about God conveyed by this parental image. For other persons, a masculine image of God presents gender problems. Though references to God as Father in the ministry of Jesus intend to communicate a potential for intimacy rather than exalt masculinity, some individuals find the gender designation of God more disturbing than enlightening. Sensitivity to potential problems in various biblical references to God assures efforts to move behind a specific image of God in a scriptural text to discover the larger truth about God as compassionate Creator and Redeemer.

A similar attentiveness to word meanings becomes crucial for an accurate understanding of the New Testament's message regarding salvation. Though various writers use the same words to describe the experience of salvation, these writers do not use these words in the same manner. A failure to recognize the different meanings of the words used to describe salvation results in a misunderstanding of this fundamental spiritual experience.

Faith and works. Some people suggest that two different schools of thought on salvation vied with each other within the primitive Christian community. One, following Paul, emphasized salvation by faith alone. The other, devoted to James, stressed the importance of faith and works. Both views on salvation claimed the authority of biblical truth.

A surface look at key Scripture passages verifies schism in the early church's understanding of salvation. Paul completely dismissed any concept of salvation on the basis of personal works, using the experience of Abraham to illustrate the accuracy of his belief. The apostle from Tarsus wrote of a person dependent upon faith alone, "His faith is reckoned as righteousness" (Romans 4:5). But James appears to contradict Paul's view, emphasizing salvation's dependence upon works and citing precisely the same experience in Abraham's life to substantiate his belief. James wrote, "A man is justified by works and not by faith alone" (James 2:24). The writings of both Paul and James come to us as the Word of God.

More than historical accuracy about an ancient ideological conflict is at stake here. What are we to believe about salvation? Does our righteousness arise out of personal effort or only as a result of God's grace? Look carefully at each writer's use of the key words *faith* and *works*. A thorough word study erases even an appearance of conflict between Paul and James on the question of salvation and demonstrates the complementary nature of their teachings.

In the writings of Paul, *faith* means absolute commitment, trust. Paul chose the term *works* to describe acts of compliance with religious law. Thus, the apostle forcefully declared that salvation cannot be earned by keeping the law. Salvation is a gift from God, an act of grace. Salvation is by faith alone. James equated *faith* with orthodoxy, a proper intellectual affirmation of various religious propositions. He used the term *works* to describe acts of goodness, the kind of actions normally associated with practical Christianity. James rejected outright any concept of salvation based upon verbal confessions and mental assertions alone, insisting that salvation involves behavior as well as belief.

Consider the fruits of this brief word study. Both Paul and James recognized that *faith* must mean trust—an absolute commitment to the person of Christ. For each writer, *faith* involved more than an assertion of the mind, confession of the lips, or legal action. Neither Paul nor James conceived of an individual's earning the right to salvation. At the same time, both writers recognized that when a person accepts the lordship of Christ, every facet of that person's life reflects this commitment. Trust in Christ inevitably results in Christlike actions.

No schism rocked the early church on the matter of salvation. Two major witnesses to the meaning of salvation spoke with unity and power. Salvation is by faith alone. This salvation always results in faithfulness. Belief in Christ finds expression in behavior patterned after the life of Christ.

Justification and righteousness. Important word pictures such as *justification* and *righteousness*, so prominent in the literature of Paul, no longer effectively reveal God's nature to everybody. These first-century images find no suitable point of contact in a contemporary mentality. The word pictures derive from a court of law. We understand that. However, we associate an impartial judge with a court of law, an officer of justice dispassionately listening to arguments before making a decision about a person's guilt or innocence. That picture does not square with the nature of God as revealed in Jesus.

God qualifies as a judge in the sense of one who passes judgment. But God is by no means dispassionate or impartial. God displays a bias toward those in need of judgment, eager to pronounce all acceptable, abounding more in grace than justice. Also, God's ultimate judgment about any person comes not on the basis of the deeds of the one on trial but on the basis of the grace of the judge. The issue is not legalism but grace.

A sense of familiarity can hinder our understanding of a passage of Scripture. Most of us assume we know the meaning of familiar words and images in the Bible. However, as noted above, what we think a text means may differ significantly from the true meaning of that text. No substitute exists for discovering the real substance of a biblical writer's words and images.

What is the immediate setting of this text?

Most biblical texts have more than one setting. Knowing something of the various settings of a text has importance for understanding the meaning of that text and seeing its relevance for our lives.

Consider, for example, narratives in the Hebrew Scriptures. Many of these circulated in three or four distinctly different realms prior to being incorporated into a particular piece of literature. Here is what happened. Particular historical circumstances gave rise to the stories in the Pentateuch. Memories of these circumstances took the form of stories circulated among the nomadic tribes of Israel. Sitting around campfires at night and passing time during daily excursions, parents intrigued their children with tales of their ancestors. Eventually, prompted by impulses from God, people began to write down their memories of various episodes in which God interacted with Israel. Finally, others incorporated these recorded stories into a singular statement of Israel's history and faith.

Not only does each biblical story have meaning within itself; the reason why people preserved the story and retold it in another time and place also has meaning. Students of these ancient stories gain insights both from a Scripture writer's incorporation, interpretation, and application of a specific tale into a piece of literature as well as from the meaning of that tale in the situation that originally gave rise to it and in the various circumstances through which it traveled on the way to taking a written form.

A situation of multiple settings applies also to many of the materials in the New Testament, especially to records related to Jesus. Obviously each statement or story from Jesus originally developed in the course of his ministry. Jesus spoke to specific audiences and acted in unique situations characterized by particular needs. Memories of these experiences lingered in the conversations and discourses of people like Peter and Matthew. Only later, often years later, did some thoughtful person in the early church—again under the impulse of God—recall a specific word from Jesus that addressed a concern or proved helpful to a situation in that church. Such an application of a comment from Jesus to a more contemporary situation both preserved and interpreted Jesus' original remark. Later still, a Gospel writer drew from both the oral tradition about Jesus' teachings and from the church's use of those materials to record comments from Jesus of importance for his specific time, interests, and mission.

Readers of the Gospels encounter statements from Jesus that passed through numerous settings by means of a variety of media. In each instance, the meaning of a story about Jesus or a statement from Jesus has been filtered through the peculiar historical circumstances that stand between the original setting in which Jesus first spoke or acted and the literary context in which the material appears in the New Testament.

In every age, cultural conditions and historical situations affect people's interpretations and applications of sacred truths. The powerful dynamic of that principle can be observed within the Scriptures themselves. Changing circumstances altered the manner in which people of faith interpreted enduring principles. Said another way, the historical setting of a biblical passage significantly colors the sentiments expressed in that passage. One illustration will suffice to make this point.

How to relate properly to the government was a constant concern among the people of God. Yet, counsel regarding this relationship varies significantly throughout the Bible. Changing historical circumstances produced different points of view regarding the nature of government and the role of God's people in relation to government. Ancient Israelites made little distinction between religion and government. Once these people inhabited a land of their own, established a government they considered to be dictated by God, and recognized leaders they believed to be chosen by God, faith and politics merged. According to the conventional wisdom of Israel, God governed the nation through kings, judges, and other officials designated by God. Most Israelites made no attempt to separate their fidelity to the government from their religious devotion to God.

Obviously, things changed. By the advent of the New Testament era, Rome ruled the holy city in which the temple stood as well as the territory around it. Though few, if any, Jewish people viewed the Roman government and its officials as elected by God, most maintained a profound respect for government leaders, viewing the institution of government as a provision of God. Paul commended civil government with spiritual enthusiasm. Writing to people who lived in the shadow of Caesar's palace, rejoicing in the "peace of Rome," and benefiting from the accomplishments of Roman law and enterprise, Paul praised government officials in his letter called Romans. Countering any residue of antigovernment sentiment in the Christian church and encouraging responsible citizenship among Christian individuals, Paul referred to government authorities as "ministers of God" (Romans 13:1-7).

Paul's comments on government did not assign ultimate authority to this social institution or call for unconditional allegiance to it. In his letters to the Corinthians, the apostle from Tarsus acknowledged government's secondary authority (1 Corinthians 6:1-8) and limited wisdom (2:8). However, Paul summoned Christians to respect the government as an instrument for good and to pray for government leaders as servants of justice. The political climate complemented the apostle's positive counsel.

Such was not the case when the book of Revelation appeared. In sharp contrast to Paul's affirmation of the government, the author of the Revelation to John labeled the government "a beast" (Revelation 13:1-8). Respect for the Roman emperor had deteriorated into worship of this civil sovereign. By the time of Domitian's reign, every citizen was required to burn incense to "the godhead" Caesar and to declare "Caesar is Lord." When Christians refused to participate in the politics of idolatry, the government turned on them with violent persecution. In Revelation, as in Romans, the author's words about government reflect the historical situation in which he wrote. A good government worthy of praise had gone bad, really bad. An institution willed by God had become an instrument of gross evil. Little wonder John's words about civil authority differ dramatically from the statements of Paul.

The Gospels record a statement from Jesus that represents a normative view regarding Christians' relations to government. Ambivalent attitudes toward the state abounded. Complaints about an intrusive foreign power and seemingly excessive taxation

existed alongside gratitude for stability, peace, and good sys-
tems of transportation. When asked about recognizing the
authority of government as a potential conflict with maintain-
ing loyalty to God, Jesus admonished people to give to the
government all that rightly belonged to the government—obedience to laws, payment of taxes, and the like—and to give to
God that which belongs to God alone—absolute obedience,
ultimate authority, worship, and selfless devotion. Jesus voiced
a respect for government tempered by a healthy recognition of
the limits to government's power.

Historical circumstances conditioned interpretations of
God's word about a healthy relationship to civil authority.
Throughout the Scriptures, government receives attention as a
divine provision for social order. However, estimates of the
inherent goodness of this institution vary dramatically according to the nature of the government in power at any one time.
Christians should always pray for those in seats of power, but
blind allegiance and unconditional service belong to God alone.

Where does this particular passage stand in the whole sweep of the Bible's message?

The location of a passage in the Bible significantly affects both
the interpretation and application of that passage. The relationship between a passage and the ministry of Jesus—particularly
the teachings of Jesus—is of crucial importance. Though Jesus
should not be read back into the Hebrew Scriptures (a practice
called *eisegesis*), the Old Testament should be read in light of the
life and ministry of Jesus.

Jesus is the ultimate revelation of God, thus, the sovereign
criterion for evaluating the rest of the Scriptures. When the
impetus of a particular text runs contrary to the focus of Jesus'
teachings, serious questions should be raised regarding the
validity of that text for contemporary believers. For example,
consider the psalmist's prayer regarding his enemies:

> Happy shall he be who takes your little ones
> and dashes them against the rock!
> —Psalm 137:9

This prayer is totally out of sync with Jesus' model ("Forgive us our debts as we forgive our debtors"; Matthew 6:12, NRSV) and his mandate ("Love your enemies and pray for those who persecute you"; Matthew 5:44). Jesus replaced retaliation with initiatives of forgiveness and reconciliation. Jesus, not a writer who lived centuries prior to the supreme revelation of God, sets the proper faith agenda for our responses to enemies and hurtful acts.

Early Christians branded Marcion as a heretic for postulating that the Bible reveals two different Gods—one in the Old Testament and one in the New Testament. Actually, many people through the ages silently have suspected what Marcion openly declared. How could the God who sent Jesus as the Prince of Peace, filled Jesus with a message of forgiveness, and commissioned followers of Jesus as ministers of reconciliation commission the Israelites to capture the city of Amalek and kill all its residents? Set side by side, pertinent passages related to these truths seem to reveal two different deities. Frankly, not all of the Old Testament squares with the teachings of Jesus.

Covering a vast period of time, the Bible contains multiple levels of understanding God. Prior to the perfect revelation of God in Christ, personal interpretations of events passed for divine revelation. At times, the people in Israel confused nationalism and self-interest with God's will. The same God worked in both the old and new Scriptures. However, not all of those prior to Christ understood God with the clarity of those who knew God through Christ. Thus, some passages of Scripture reflect a partial understanding or a gross misunderstanding of God's will and appear inconsistent with the mind of Christ. Bible students do well not to assign the same level of importance and contemporary application to those passages as they give to texts that reflect the full glory of God as seen in Christ.

Keep in mind that we know the Jesus who enlightens our interpretation of various texts only through other texts and their interpreters. New Testament writers present a variety of pictures of Jesus. Each enhances our understanding of Jesus, though Jesus is greater than any one depiction of him. Despite diverse perspectives on Jesus, certain qualities prevail in all descriptions of Jesus—love, mercy, forgiveness. These traits (qualities of Christlike character) establish the norm by which the authority of other passages of Scripture is determined. Any biblical text in conflict with the truth incarnate in Jesus must yield to the superiority of Jesus.

Asking Important Questions

Once I start to understand the nature of a particular Scripture text (through answering the questions asked above), I am ready to raise important questions of my own about the general meaning and specific application of that passage. Answers to these questions form a bridge that spans the centuries to connect ancient words with contemporary situations. Suddenly a truth commended by a person in the distant past leaps across time to confront me with a word from God for today. The questions I ask follow.

What is the subject of this text?

Be careful here. Establishing the subject of a text requires more than a quick perusal of the words in a passage and a snap judgment concerning the "obvious" topic to which these words point. What seems readily apparent about a text does not always turn out to be the real subject of that text. Many Scripture passages contain much more—or much less—than meets a reader's eye at first glance.

For example, many people unfortunately consider the Ten Commandments to be a compendium of fundamental prohibitions intended to restrict life and regulate religion. Such a characterization of the Decalogue misses both its subject matter and its spirit. The Ten Commandments grow out of the love of God, who graciously delivers people out of slavery (Exodus 20:2), and stand as God's affirmations of the best way to live in freedom. Rather than restrictions on life, these commandments point the way to maturation and fulfillment in life. Each "no" ("thou shalt not") derives from a higher "yes." God prohibits murder, adultery, and theft because God knows that life goes better when people respect the sanctity of individuals, fidelity in relationships, and honesty in work and words. The Ten

Commandments define basic qualities essential to a good life individually and socially.

A more expansive statement of the good life intended by God occurs early in the teachings of Jesus and carries the title the Sermon on the Mount. Here again some people misread this masterful collection of teachings couched in grace as a new legal brief based on an updated summation of God's law. Wrong. A thoughtful consideration of the Sermon on the Mount leads us into the realm of God's rule where intention is as important as action, retaliation is swallowed up in grace, and loving communion with God takes precedence over conformity to religious rituals. Jesus described the bountiful joy that wells up in God in response to a person's life of humility, mercy, purity, and peacemaking (see the Beatitudes in Matthew 5:3-12). The subject of the Sermon on the Mount is the nature of a life committed to the will of God. Grace, not law, occupies the center of its focus. Rather than prescribing prohibitions and restrictions, Jesus spoke of liberation and redemption in life. Here is a portrait of the joys and responsibilities of a person devoted to loving and serving God.

Misunderstanding the subject of certain texts blunts sensitivity, blinds consciousness, and leads to radical misperceptions of God's intentions. Accurately establishing the subject of a passage is essential for getting in touch and staying in touch with the truths in that passage. We will take a look at a few biblical texts often substantially misunderstood because of inaccurate judgments about their subjects.

Prediction for the future or promise for the present (Isaiah 9:6)? We read ancient Scriptures in light of what we know of Christ. Consequently, we sometimes see Christ as the subject of a prophetic passage in the Hebrew Scriptures that was intended to speak to the people among whom it arose. The text points to a figure who looks like and sounds like Christ.

> For to us a child is born,
>   to us a son is given;
> and the government will be upon his shoulder,
>   and his name will be called
> "Wonderful Counselor, Mighty God,
>   Everlasting Father, Prince of Peace."

The prophet Isaiah described the kind of ideal leadership needed by the people of Israel after the overthrow of their foreign oppressors. Isaiah probably composed this material as a coronation liturgy for a new king. His lofty words instructed and encouraged his contemporaries, who were eager to experience the care and provisions of God. Without question, Jesus ultimately fulfilled this text in a manner unachievable by anyone else. However, the true subject of the text was a new king for Isaiah's day—a subject with great significance for its original hearers' understanding of the compassionate intention of God.

Where will the great war be fought (Revelation 16:12-16)? Bible teachers in the church of my childhood made no distinction between their interpretations of apocalyptic literature, prophecy, and historical narratives. Thus, they read this passage in Revelation ("And they assembled them at the place that in Hebrew is called Armageddon," verse 16) as a warning of an actual battle that would occur in the future, probably in our lifetime. Subsequently, I invested youthful concern in what life would be like in the wake of this ultimate war. Every time a crisis developed in the Middle East, my anxiety level rose as leaders in my church pointed to the possibility of an imminent battle of Armageddon.

As I indicated previously, to read apocalyptic literature as a chart for the future is to misunderstand its subject matter. God inspired these highly symbolic materials to minister to people faced by overwhelming problems. The author of Revelation wrote not about a major military battle scheduled for eruption in my day but about pressing problems in his time and how God would prevail over them.

The subject of Revelation 16:12-16 is a conflict between God's truth and evil lies or, as one writer put it, "the gospel" and "the badspell." No amount of military might could assure victory in this battle. Those early Christians who constituted a minority in a society lashing out at them with persecution took hope in the content of this passage. Here was assurance that God's truth would prevail regardless of all appearances to the contrary.

Should we take poverty for granted (Mark 14:3-9)? Early in the week of Jesus' crucifixion, a woman in Bethany anointed Jesus with costly oil. Some disciples complained about the extravagance of the act, arguing that the costly ointment could have been sold for a high price and the proceeds given to the poor. Jesus defended the woman's action. He observed that people could give to the poor anytime—"You always have the poor with you" (Mark 14:7)—though he would soon be absent. A close look at the context as well as the content of this passage reveals its primary subject. Jesus commended an extravagant display of affection as proper preparation for his passion and a meaningful display of devotion. Moderation has no place in Christian commitment and authentic love.

The contrast between the imminent absence of Jesus and the ongoing presence of the poor served to highlight the urgency and importance of the woman's action. In no sense should the statement from Jesus be considered a rationale for passivity regarding poverty or a prediction of the impossibility of social reform aimed at the elimination of poverty. This passage is not about poverty. The central truth in this episode from the life of Jesus emphasizes how to love God and serve Jesus, acts that elsewhere in the Gospels inevitably involve ministries to the poor.

What does this text mean to me?

Prior to answering this question, a reader may need to raise another: What presuppositions affect my ability to understand the relevance of this passage for my life? In other words, can I discern what this text means to me? No one reads the Bible devoid of basic assumptions. Identifying our assumptions related to the Bible makes us aware of how presuppositions can blind us or deafen us to a text's meaning for us.

Ernest Best identified both the sources and the content of a few common assumptions that exert major influence on many people's understanding of the Bible's meaning for their lives. First in importance are presuppositions about the nature of the Bible itself. Questions to ask in identifying these presuppositions include the following: Is the Bible inspired? Is it infallible? Can revelations of God be found outside the Bible? Second, assumptions precipitated by the nature of a person's faith affect biblical interpretation. An examination of such assumptions may involve self-interrogation that includes these inquiries: Do miracles happen? Does God change the course of nature and intervene in world history? Does God have a purpose for every life, for my life? Is Jesus essential to salvation? Third, presuppositions shaped by the culture in which people live affect biblical understanding. Interpreters do well to examine their conclusions in response to questions like these: Are science and faith in conflict? Can technology solve most of the world's problems? What are people's basic rights? Is the political process off-limits to the people of God? How we answer these questions determines how we do biblical interpretation.[2]

Scriptural interpretation occurs as a personal experience, but it should not be a purely subjective exercise. What I think about or say about a text is not nearly so important as how that text addresses me and what it says. To hear, see, and understand what a text means for me requires that I allow the text to address my mind as well as my spirit, to engage my reason as well as my emotions. Out of a thoroughgoing dialogue with a text, I come to a realization of its truth and that truth's meaning for me. Two lines from J. A. Bengel printed on one of the front pages of my old Nestle's Greek New Testament are lodged in my memory. They continue to serve me well as I work at understanding the Bible:

> Thy whole self apply to the text.
> The whole text apply to thyself.[3]

How have other Christians interpreted this text?

Individuals interpret the Bible. However, biblical interpretation is not a private affair. Accuracy in interpretation requires the guidance of the Holy Spirit and the collective wisdom of the people of God.

The Bible is a book of the church. Through the centuries, the church has both preserved and interpreted the Bible. The God who inspired the Bible guided the church. Divine inspiration

---

2. Ernest Best, *From Text to Sermon* (Atlanta: John Knox, 1978), 97-98.

3. *Novum Testamentum Graece*, ed. Eberhard Nestle (Stuttgart: Privileg. Wurtt, Bibelanstalt, n,d.).

did not cease once God's revelation was reduced to words on parchment. God's Spirit continued to enlighten the minds of people of faith who studied the inspired Scriptures. God's Spirit extends that gift into the present.

Interpreting the Bible is a never-ending exercise. Cumulative wisdom regarding the Scriptures is of major importance. Because all interpreters bring presuppositions to their work and reflect the influence of their cultures, blind spots develop during certain periods of time, and major omissions, if not errors, in interpretation occur. However, every generation of biblical studies builds on and reacts to studies in previous periods. A pertinent truth overlooked by interpreters in one age gains prominence in another age.

Personally, when I am struggling with a text, I like to know how that text has been treated by church people in three or four significant periods of history. I find help in looking at the interpretive work of an early church leader like Augustine, one of the Reformers such as Martin Luther or John Calvin, an influential preacher of the last century like John Wesley, one of the formative theologians of the first half of the twentieth century such as Karl Barth, and a leading thinker in contemporary Christendom. Frequently female commentators provide invaluable textual insights and applications missed by males. Likewise, works from students of the Bible living in Third World nations offer perspectives on truth of which commentators in more affluent settings seem incapable. I also find it beneficial to read textual treatments written by persons who espouse a theological perspective very different from mine.

Few of us have access to libraries stocked with unlimited numbers of Bible commentaries. However, we often can get hold of two or three major works on a particular book of the Bible. A quick look at how different commentators have interpreted a passage can greatly aid our understanding of that passage.

What is the theology of this text?

The Bible is a theological book, not an elaborate treatise on one expansive theology but a compendium of various theological insights that marked the communities of Judaism and Christianity. Faith preceded the Bible. Through the Bible, practitioners of faith bore witness to the nature and purpose of God *according to their understanding*. Thus, several different theological viewpoints can be found in the Bible. Common to all, however, was the intention of nurturing people's relationship with God. The author of the Fourth Gospel, for example, left no doubt about the nature of the material he brought together as a Gospel: "These are written that you may believe that Jesus is the Christ, the Son of God, and that believing you may have life in his name" (John 20:31).

Theological bias causes major problems in biblical interpretation. Everyone approaches Scripture from a theological point of view—informed or uninformed, rational or emotional, sound or flawed. Honestly engaging a biblical text necessitates openly acknowledging personal theological assumptions and working carefully not to read these preferences into the meaning of a given passage. The goal is to allow every biblical passage to speak for itself, to elaborate its own theology.

Several different theologies appear throughout the Scriptures—one building on another, one contradicting another, one superseding others. Frankly, the theological mixture found in the Bible can baffle an impatient interpreter. The most helpful method of biblical interpretation considers the whole of the Bible and studies its individual parts, permitting various theologies to converse with each other. Truth emerges out of the affirmations, agreements, contradictions, and rejections that develop out of the interchange between various theological points of view.

The earliest theology found in the Bible attributed everything to God. A writer, often referred to as the "Deuteronomic historian," in deference to his belief in the sovereignty of God, recognized no secondary causes related to circumstances. Positing that the sovereign God controls all of history, this writer explained everything that happened as the will of God. Occasionally even pagan acts, deeds of retaliatory anger, greedy vengeance, and coldhearted military strategy were attributed to the directive of God. The author of 1 Samuel wrote, "Thus says the LORD of hosts, 'I will punish the Amalekites for what they did in opposing the Israelites. . . . go and attack Amalek, and utterly destroy all that they have; do not spare them, but kill both man and woman, child and infant'" (15:2-3, NRSV).

According to this simple theology, good reaps rewards immediately, even as evil prompts quick punishment. Proponents of such thought automatically concluded that people battling disease, hardships, or tragic circumstances had brought these on themselves by sinful behavior. Conversely, prosperity indicated God's pleasure with a person. Individual or national success was a sure sign of righteousness. But eventually people questioned this theology. Not everything seemed to square with its basic propositions. Sometimes good people suffered. Apart from any recognizable reason for divine punishment, hardships hurt individuals characterized by exemplary piety. Also, good things happened in the lives of bad people. Greed worked. Loveless power prevailed. Thoughtful people began to question a moral justification for all that transpired in people's lives and surmised that maybe not every historical development ought to be considered God's action.

The Old Testament book of Job, built around the tragic life of a faithful religious figure well known in Jewish history, elaborated an important, new theological initiative. The author-theologian challenged the idea that hurtful events in a person's life signal immoral behavior and that prosperity always rewards goodness. The theology of the book of Job recognized a complexity in life that defies simple explanations for all circumstances. At its center pulsates an affirmation that God remains with people in both the best and worst moments of their lives. Subsequently, a faithful relationship with God needs no validation outside itself. In the face of taunts to curse God, Job voiced the attitude of a faithful relationship with God, "Naked I came from my mother's womb, and naked shall I return; the LORD gave, and the LORD has taken away; blessed be the name of the LORD" (1:21).

Other theologies appear in the Hebrew Scriptures. A theology of conquest accompanied Israel's invasion of the Promised Land. The somewhat comic book of Jonah presented a revolutionary (and highly controversial) theology of mission—universal in scope. Isaiah detailed a theology of servanthood and hope.

The prophet Amos altered the prevailing theological understanding of the "day of the LORD" as he explored the relationship
between God's wrath and God's love.

Virtually all students of the Bible recognize the prevalence of
Paul's theology in the New Testament. Around the core con-
cepts of freedom and justification by faith, Paul wrote of the
grace of God, the justice of God, the wrath of God, and the
greatest of them all—the love of God that finds expression
among the people of God. Not everyone so readily recognizes
different theologies among the Gospel writers in the New Testament. A careful reading of Matthew, Mark, Luke, and John
reveals that each author worked with a distinct theology. All
made literary decisions about material to be included in their
books on the basis of individual theological convictions. An
examination of differences in the texts of the various Gospels
exposes distinctions between the theological perspectives of the
respective authors. Each addressed in his own manner the
meaning of Jesus and the significance of what God was doing
in the world through Jesus.

In a careful study comparing the resurrection narratives in
the first three Gospels, Norman Perrin found three distinct
theologies of the resurrection.[4] All three evangelists answered
the same question: What does it mean to say that Jesus Christ is
risen from the dead? But each evangelist responded to that
inquiry in his own manner. For Mark, the resurrection of Jesus
meant an ability for people to experience the ultimate reality of
Jesus in everyday occurrences—to find Jesus transforming both
the world and their daily lives in the world. For Matthew, the
resurrection of Jesus made it possible for people to experience
Jesus and to be transformed by Jesus in the life of the church.
Luke believed the Resurrection created a potential for people to
imitate the example of Jesus and to benefit from the inspiration
and power of the Spirit of God.

In a sense, each of the Synoptic writers developed a pastoral
theology. None developed doctrine for the sake of doctrine.
Each described the benefits for believers inherent in Jesus'

---

4. Norman Perrin, *The Resurrection according to Matthew, Mark, and Luke* (Philadelphia: Fortress, 1977).

Easter action. Mark wanted his readers to experience God in their daily lives and assured them of that possibility. Matthew desired for his readers to recognize the church as a fellowship in which Jesus would sustain their lives as believers. Luke described Jesus as the first Christian in order to declare that the Spirit that empowered Jesus will empower all who believe in and follow him.

Recognizing the theology reflected in a text throws helpful light on an exploration of the meaning of that text. Details in a passage of Scripture that otherwise might perplex an interpreter take on significant meaning when viewed as a part of a particular theological point of view.

Does the truth of this text stand alone, or does it need the balance of other biblical texts?

An old axiom asserts that a person can prove anything by the Bible. In actual fact, across the years, people have cited the Bible as their authority for burning witches, practicing slavery, killing infidels, ignoring the poor, defending racism, violating human rights, and declaring war. Currently a political ideology called *reconstructionism* advocates considering a return to the so-called biblical morality of executing adulterers, homosexuals, people who teach false doctrines, and juveniles who continue delinquent behavior. Startling conclusions take shape when people lift passages from their context in the Bible and posit the meaning of these passages in isolation from any consideration of truths contained in other biblical texts. Serious distortions of truth emerge from this method of Bible study. The will of God can be cited as the motivation for actions completely contrary to the revealed nature of God, actions actually prohibited in the Word of God.

Though the Bible has many parts, its unity prevails. No one text can claim the importance that belongs to the whole sweep of biblical truth. As a matter of fact, any passage in the Bible is best understood when considered in relation to other passages in the Bible. Each text may present an important aspect of the revelation of God. However, confronting the full revelation of God in the Bible requires familiarity with all the Bible.

Viewed in isolation, virtually every point of view apparent in the Bible faces a contrary point of view also integral to the Bible. Compare the psalmist's venomous prayer for the demise of his enemies, "Contend, O LORD, with those who contend with me. . . . Let their way be dark and slippery. . . . Let ruin come upon them unawares! . . . let them fall therein to ruin! Then my soul shall rejoice in the LORD" (Psalm 35:1-9), with Jesus' admonition, "Love your enemies and pray for those who persecute you" (Matthew 5:44). When a jailer in Philippi asked, "What must I do to be saved?" Paul and others answered, "Believe in the Lord Jesus, and you will be saved" (Acts 16:30-31). Elsewhere, though, various texts link salvation to baptism: "Be baptized, and have your sins washed away" (Acts 22:16, NRSV); "Peter said to them, 'Repent, and be baptized every one of you in the name of Jesus Christ so that your sins may be forgiven'" (Acts 2:38, NRSV); and "As many of you as were baptized into Christ have clothed yourselves with Christ" (Galatians 3:27, NRSV). Beware of interpreting any biblical text in isolation from the whole of God's revelation in the Bible.

What does the Bible say about slavery? Much of it appears to take slavery for granted. Thoughtful people like Moses, Jesus, and Paul considered slavery a social given. Across the years, people have cited numerous biblical texts to support the perpetuation of bondage for certain segments of humankind: "You are cursed, and some of you shall always be slaves" (Joshua 9:23); "Slaves, be obedient to those who are your earthly masters, with fear and trembling, in singleness of heart, as to Christ" (Ephesians 6:5). However, the total impact of the Bible counters the slavery-supporting implications of specific texts.

The Creation accounts point to the dignity and worth of all persons created in the image of God. The God of creation is the God of the Exodus. Throughout the Hebrew Scriptures, God reveals a bias toward persons held in captivity of any kind and a penchant for providing deliverance. God's great prophets rail against oppression. Similarly, in the New Testament, Jesus begins his public ministry announcing a commitment to "proclaim release to the captives" (Luke 4:18). Freedom for every person forms the center of the story of redemption. Paul recognized that a relationship with Christ eradicates structures of superiority and inferiority between all people—"For freedom Christ has set us free; stand fast therefore, and do not submit again to a yoke of slavery" (Galatians 5:1). Thus, the thrust of the Bible transcends specific texts in the Bible to challenge slavery and encourage freedom. God's word of liberation is superior to the culture of slavery in which that word was first revealed.

When we weigh contradictory texts against each other in search of an authoritative word, wisdom guides us to give prominence to the passage that stands closest to the life and teachings of Jesus. Consider repetition as well. A principle or a truth meriting obedience should have more than one text to support it. The ultimate validity of a particular text stems from that text's compatibility and consistency with the whole sweep of biblical truth.

Where and how does this text intersect contemporary society?

In his Warrack Lectures on preaching, James Cleland described the Word of God as an ellipse with two focal points. On one side of the ellipse, he placed a biblical text, and on the other, some aspect of the contemporary situation. Cleland suggested that the word of God always emerges from (and involves) a biblical text in interaction with a contemporary situation.[5] This approach to interpretation is the practical corollary of the theological doctrine of the Incarnation—the Word becomes flesh again.

At first glance, many biblical texts seem totally out of touch with the world in which we live. Virtually every biblical text confronts us with a world very different from the one we know. For that reason, people often make the mistake either of writing off the biblical situation as totally irrelevant or of attempting, as an act of great faith, to impose that situation on today's world, much like forcing a square peg into a round hole. Neither of these reactions is beneficial or necessary.

A crucial first act in biblical interpretation involves distinguishing between time-bound and timeless dimensions of a

---

5. James T. Cleland, *Preaching to Be Understood* (Nashville: Abingdon Press, 1965), 33-58.

given text. Biblical situations often differ dramatically from biblical principles. Not infrequently, biblical principles stand in judgment of the sociocultural contexts in which they were revealed. Obedience to the Bible involves no obligation to reproduce the specific sociocultural situation encountered in a passage; rather, the obligation is application of and conformity to the enduring principle (or principles) revealed in that situation.

The truth of the Bible always unfolds in a specific setting. Contextual understandings of that truth reflect nuances of the prevailing culture at the time. However, biblical truth transcends historical circumstances and intersects the world in which we live. We have not properly finished with a biblical text until we recognize its impact upon our world generally and upon our personal lives particularly.

Questions often dominate the intersection between a biblical text and our world. Reading about the Israelites' dance around the golden calf at the foot of the mountain while Moses received God's revelation of the Decalogue on top of the mountain spurs me to consider what golden calves of superstition continue to attract loyalty in close proximity to claims of authentic faith. Pondering Jeremiah's complaints about being caught between faith and politics makes me wonder about the dangerous fusion of political partisanship and spiritual convictions obvious in so many camps today.

Promises, assurance, and encouragement may also occupy that same point of meeting between the two worlds. To read of Jesus walking on water to reach his disciples caught in a storm on the lake of Gennesaret says to me that Jesus seeks us out amid the storms that thunder into our lives so that now as well as then he may offer comfort. Jesus' high priestly prayer for the church assures me that efforts toward unity in Christendom qualify as partial answers to Jesus' prayer.

A vision of responsibilities may also arise at the touch point between a biblical text and our present situation. After telling the story of the good Samaritan, Jesus commissioned listeners to follow the Samaritan's example. That makes me responsible for people in the ditches that cut through my town. Reading of Jesus feeding the multitudes pricks my conscience about my role in feeding the hungry masses in our world. I cannot think about Jesus' blessing of the peacemakers without concerning myself with the things that make for peace in our society. Out of dialogue between a biblical text and the present moment, the word of God appears with power and promise. A recognition of that reality leads to the final question in this discussion.

What does this text demand of me in terms of compliance or obedience?

A friend offered an interesting response to an invitation to dinner one Saturday evening. After explaining that she really needed to stay at home and study the Sunday school lesson she would teach the next day, the woman observed, "But this is an easy lesson; it's about the sixth commandment. Everybody knows what that means, and it doesn't have much importance for my class." Well, what does the divine prohibition against killing mean in terms of obedience? Is the sixth commandment about all killing or only murder? Does our obedience to this commandment in any way affect our thoughts and actions related to war, abortion, and starvation?

Bible study is not an end in itself. The goal of Bible study involves action as well as more knowledge. Understanding the meaning of a biblical text serves as a prelude to implementing the truth of that text in our lives. Conscientious interpreters of the Bible move quickly to incorporate the truths of the Bible into the ebb and flow of personal experience.

Jesus' words about forgiveness constitute both a gift and a demand. Nothing we can do exempts us from God's forgiveness. However, we are to share the gift of forgiveness. Indeed, Jesus indicated that people who are forgiven most will be the most forgiving toward others. I find forgiveness, when it is fully understood, to be a very controversial subject—not the assurance of God's forgiveness but the commission for us to be forgiving. Recently, after I explored the meaning of forgiveness in a sermon, a gentleman said to me as he exited the sanctuary, "You mean God expects me to forgive that ... [expletive deleted] who treated my daughter so terribly?" This man had made contact with the demands of the Bible on his life.

A phrase from Paul also comes to mind in this regard. Writing to the Philippians, the apostle urged, "Live your life in a manner worthy of the gospel of Christ" (1:27, NRSV). What a challenge! The comprehensive implications of this admonition take on even more stringent meaning when readers discover that the phrase "manner of life" (as the RSV translates it) comes from the word *politeusthe*, from which we get the word *politics*. The apostle indicated that our politics, like the rest of our lives, should be "worthy of the gospel of Christ." Obedience to that commission involves practicing responsible citizenship and engaging in political action as well as more traditional acts associated with Christian devotion.

Quiet Listening

Exercises billed as Bible studies often degenerate into a prolonged exchange of personal opinions. A familiar pattern unfolds. After reading a passage of Scripture, a Sunday school teacher or another study leader asks the question, "What do you think this text means?" Participants offer off-the-cuff statements such as, "Well, to me, this was something valid in the past that has no meaning for the present"; "I don't see how anyone could think this passage has anything to do with loving people who are not kind to our nation"; or "The way I see it, that writer didn't want us to give up our pursuit of financial affluence." Swapping personal opinions about the Bible passes for grappling with the truth of the Bible.

Caution! Apart from the discipline of answering and asking the kinds of text-oriented questions discussed above, uninformed reactions take the place of meaningful interpretation in relation to a text. People's thoughts about a passage in the Bible take priority over discovering the thought in that text. The difference between the two postures is crucial. Sharing individual sentiments about the Scriptures is a poor substitute for seriously studying the Scriptures.

Bible study involves the Bible's addressing us much more than our addressing the Bible. What we think a text means cannot take the place of what a text means. How we assess the Bible pales in significance to how the Bible assesses us. Once the preparatory work of biblical interpretation has been done—asking and answering questions about a passage—a time arrives when we cease working on a text and allow that text to work on us. If we never fall silent before a passage and listen carefully to that passage, we are unlikely to hear the word of God addressing us through that passage. And, if we are not going to hear the word of God in the Bible, why bother with the Bible?

The whole point of Bible study is discovery. We come away from encounters with the Scriptures confidently declaring, as did Jeremiah to King Zedekiah, there is a word from the Lord. Through the content of the Bible, God confronts us with a word by means of which God can transform our lives and redeem our world.

CHAPTER 4

Beyond Belief

A story I heard as a student sensitized me to the dangerous possibility of separating belief in the Bible from living the Bible. An old, well-established, all-white body of believers found its neighborhood rapidly developing into an interracial community. Uncomfortable with the transition, some people in the church pushed the idea of relocation. Others saw no problem in the new situation and argued for a recommitment to the historic site of the church's structures. In the midst of divisive debate, members of the congregation decided to resolve the issue biblically.

The church affirmed its belief in the Bible. Then, for several weeks, members of the church came together to study the Bible's teachings on the nature of the church, the challenge of ministry, and a Christian perspective on racial diversity. At the end of this period, members scheduled a business meeting in which to vote on the matter of relocation. In a period of discussion prior to the vote in the business meeting, one gentleman, who had attended all the Bible-study sessions, spoke vehemently about relocation. Prejudice, hatred, and bitterness laced his remarks. When challenged with material from the Bible, the man remarked in anger, "I don't give a damn what the Bible says; this is what I want."

To his credit, the man who spoke in the business meeting

exhibited far more candor and honesty than most people can muster when describing feelings about the Bible. Innumerable persons share this fellow's sentiments but disguise them in the language of piety or stay quiet. For many individuals, a cavernous gap separates believing the Bible confessionally from living the Bible practically. Personally, I have always found it much easier to believe correctly than to behave that way. On most days, my intentions have been impeccable even when my behavior was deplorable.

The Bible takes aim at such division within a person. The message of the Bible provides the blueprint needed to build a bridge between belief and behavior and encourages consistent travel back and forth between the two. Through narrative after narrative in the Scriptures, God calls us to know what we believe, to accept responsibility as good stewards of the mysteries of the gospel, to develop sound doctrine. By far, though, the weight of the biblical revelation falls on action—living as the people of God, following Jesus, doing the work of God. Note the explicit purpose of the Bible's promises and provisions: that the people of God "may be complete, equipped for every good work" (2 Timothy 3:17).

Beyond Belief: A Biblical Pattern

Studying the Bible is important. But Bible study alone is no substitute for living the Bible. Professing belief in scriptural truth cannot suffice for practicing that truth. Declared affirmations of a biblical doctrine do not supplant the need for quietly and consistently incorporating—incarnating—biblical beliefs through the thoughts, words, and actions of our personal lives.

The Bible presents a pattern of study and action worthy of emulation. Consider the sequence of events in an encounter between an evangelist named Philip and a eunuch from Ethiopia (Acts 8:26-40). Philip found an Ethiopian reading from the scroll of Isaiah. Impressed by the sight, Philip asked the fellow if he understood what he was reading. Immediately the man said no, "How can I [understand], unless some one guides me?" Philip accepted the challenge. He and the Ethiopian worked through various passages of the Bible together in search of understanding the biblical message. When the Ethiopian grasped the good news about God's revelation in Jesus, he wanted no delay in identifying with Christ. As the two men passed a body of water alongside the road, the Ethiopian requested baptism. Philip baptized the man.

Look at the pattern evidenced in this episode of meaningful Bible study: reading the Bible, asking for help in interpreting the Bible, moving toward an understanding of what was read, and taking action on the biblical truth discovered. An encounter with the Word of God not only informs us but inspires us to take action in response to God's Word. The Bible enables us to believe *and* to express that belief in our behavior.

The Bible and Spirituality

"Have this mind among yourselves, which is yours in Christ Jesus," Paul admonished (Philippians 2:5). Obedience to that counsel, so important for a Christian life, involves much more than learning about the Word of God—establishing the context, dates, and settings of biblical passages; exegeting texts line by line; and summarizing the teachings of the Scriptures. Developing the mind of Christ requires incorporating the Word of God as an integral part of our lives—allowing Scriptures to lodge in our minds, take up residence in our hearts, reside in our relationships, and form the substance of our conversations, decisions, and actions.

People enthusiastic about Bible study often speak of their "hunger for the Word" and dedication to "getting into the Word." Both the assumptions and intentions behind such talk merit commendation. However, getting the Word into us and allowing the Word to be active through us are goals equally, if not more, compatible with Paul's admonition. Meaningful engagements with the Bible result not only in knowledge about the Bible but a way of life based on the Bible—realizing the mind of Christ growing in us, experiencing the Word of God becoming flesh through us.

Lectio Divina

A practice called *lectio divina*—the Latin for "spiritual read-ing"—has proven to be a valuable means by which individuals allow the Bible to pervade their very beings. In addition to engaging in careful studies of the Scriptures—asking and an-swering the questions suggested in the previous chapter—indi-viduals spend quality time reading and meditating on the Scriptures, listening for the voice of God about the text and through the text.

The purpose of spiritual reading is Christian formation rather than additional information. Knowing the Bible remains impor-tant; spiritual reading in no way negates the importance of investigating and interpreting biblical texts. However, spiritual reading seeks to move people beyond a rational exercise to experience a Spirit-guided change in life that causes the en-tirety of one's being and doing to reflect the will of God. Meditating on the Scriptures, spiritual readers keep the eyes and ears of their souls open to receive God's revelation in and through various texts. As a result, an in-depth experience of the Bible accompanies a better understanding of the Bible in a person's life.

In a wonderful book on Christian spirituality, Marjorie Thompson draws from a sixth-century Benedictine tradition to outline four basic phases of spiritual reading.[1] Each aspect of the process contributes to the impact of the whole experience. Take a look.

Lectio. The word from which we derive such terms as lectionary simply means "reading." In relation to the Bible, though, it designates a special kind of reading: "reading as if you had a love letter in hand," Thompson suggests (p. 23). Both pace and openness are important. The Bible is read as if for the first time in hope of hearing something from God that is brand-new. Toward that end, a reader may remain with the same sentence for an extended period of time, reading and rereading it slowly, word by word, allowing each part of it to sink deep into the psyche.

---

1. Marjorie J. Thompson, *Soul Feast: An Invitation to the Christian Spiritual Life* (Louisville: Westminster/John Knox, 1995).

Meditatio. This term means "meditation." More than lengthy concentration, however, is involved in Bible-centered meditation. Members of the early church often chose one word from the Scriptures and repeated that word over and over throughout their activities of the day. It was a means of making that word a part of the person. Remember the image of Mary, the mother of Jesus, who in reaction to the announcement from Gabriel and subsequent events set in motion by that announcement "kept all these things, pondering them in her heart" (Luke 2:19).

Obviously meditation means more than sitting quietly and passively before a text. Intense reflection on a passage brings the words of that passage into interaction with our questions, emotions, hopes, and intentions. We see ourselves in the text and ponder the meaning of the text in us.

Oratio. Though usually associated with spoken words, this term, in relation to spiritual reading, designates words that emerge from meditations on the Scriptures. A person who has heard a word from God after reading and pondering a passage from the Bible invariably wants to respond to God. The words of such a response take form deep in the soul and find expression as a confession of joy, pain, commitment, or some other profound emotion.

Contemplatio. Thompson chose a verse from the Psalms to define *contemplatio:*

> Enough for me to keep my soul tranquil and quiet
> like a child in its mother's arms,
> as content as a child that has been weaned.
> —Psalm 131:2 (JB)

Having encountered the word of God in the Bible, meditated on it, and responded to it with silent words born deep in our beings, we come to a time to enjoy the word, to rest in it and on it, to allow the word to wash over us and to sink in us. No agenda for thought or action rules the moment. Being takes over—being in the word and being with the word in us.

Reading the Bible in this manner allows us to absorb the truth of the Scriptures and to experience the transformation which that truth brings to our lives. Encountering the Word of God leads us into the presence of the God who spoke the word. In the presence of God, we find life and we rejoice.

Praying the Bible

Communion consists of reciprocal communication. Communion with God involves both listening and speaking to God. Hearing the Word of God prompts a response—praise for God, a complaint to God, questioning God, requests of God, laments before God. But, often that response is not as easy as it may seem. At times our deepest thoughts and feelings defy verbal articulation. Wanting badly to communicate with God, we find ourselves helplessly mute in the presence of God. In such moments, we may claim the promise described by Paul—"The Spirit helps us in our weakness; for we do not know how to pray as we ought" (Romans 8:26)—and trust God's Spirit to interpret our sighs, groaning, and silence. Another alternative in those moments is to communicate with God using words from God taken from the Scriptures. We pray the Bible.

Praying the Bible need not be limited to times of spiritual trauma that rob us of words. An intense reading of a passage from the Bible may naturally draw us toward other biblical texts that we appropriate as content for our own personal prayer. Pondering Jesus' statement of self-identification built around the image of a shepherd, we begin mouthing the shepherd psalm as a prayer of faith, "The LORD is my shepherd, . . ." (Psalm 23). Similarly, heeding the counsel of the author of Hebrews who wrote, "Let us continually offer up a sacrifice of praise to God" (13:15), we embrace expressions from the psalmist, filter them through our own experience, and offer them to God as a personal declaration of delight in God, "I will praise the LORD as long as I live; I will sing praises to my God while I have being" (Psalm 146:2).

Not uncommonly a text of the Bible simply expresses our sentiments better than we can convey them ourselves. At the beginning of a service of corporate worship, I often pray the words of the psalmist, "Let the words of my mouth and the meditation of my heart be acceptable to you, O LORD" (Psalm 19:14). Spiritual perplexity spurs me to voice the succinct prayer of the man in the Gospels whose words capture perfectly what I want to say to God, "I believe; help my unbelief!" (Mark 9:24). When guilt weighs so heavy on the soul that even raising one's head is difficult, much less speaking, the confession attributed to King David provides a means of prayer without which prayer might not occur, "Have mercy on me, O God, according to thy steadfast love; . . . cleanse me from my sin! . . . I know my transgressions, and my sin is ever before me. Against thee, thee only, have I sinned, and done that which is evil in thy sight. . . . Purge me . . . wash me. . . . Fill me with joy and gladness. . . . Create in me a clean heart, O God" (Psalm 51:1-10).

Prayers abound in the Bible. Any of these prayers offered by our spiritual predecessors can bear to God the burdens, joys, questions, and affirmations of our lives. Other biblical materials provide help as well. No dimension of our experience lies beyond the Bible's ability to give substance to our prayers. Consider the following representative possibilities.

Prayers that question. "My God, my God, why hast thou forsaken me? Why art thou so far from helping me?" (Psalm 22:1); "Why dost thou hide thy face from me?" (Psalm 88:14); "I say to God, my rock: 'Why hast thou forgotten me?'" (Psalm 42:9).

Prayers of request. "Let us therefore approach the throne of grace with boldness, so that we may receive mercy and find grace to help in time of need" (Hebrews 4:16, NRSV); "Out of the depths I cry to you, O LORD. Lord, hear my voice! Let your ears be attentive to the voice of my supplications" (Psalm 130:1).

Prayers of lament. "My soul is cast down within me" (Psalm 42:6); "O LORD, how long shall I cry for help, and thou wilt not hear?" (Habakkuk 1:2); "I would speak to the Almighty, and I desire to argue my case with God" (Job 13:3); "My eyes are spent with weeping; my stomach churns" (Lamentations 2:11, NRSV).

Prayers of faith. "The life I now live in the flesh I live by faith in the Son of God" (Galatians 2:20); "The LORD is my light and my salvation; whom shall I fear? The LORD is the stronghold of my life; of whom shall I be afraid?" (Psalm 27:1); "Though I walk in the midst of trouble, you preserve me" (Psalm 138:7,

NRSV); "You have taken up my cause, O Lord, you have redeemed my life" (Lamentations 3:58, NRSV).

Prayers of petition. "Hear my cry, O God; listen to my
prayer. From the end of the earth I call to you, when my heart
is faint. Lead me to the rock that is higher than I" (Psalm 61:1-2,
NRSV); "Incline your ear, O LORD, and answer me, for I am poor
and needy" (Psalm 86:1, NRSV); "Comfort, O comfort my people" (Isaiah 40:1, NRSV).

Prayers of commitment. I will "let the word of Christ
dwell in me richly" (Colossians 3:16, NRSV); "Here am I, the
servant of the Lord; let it be with me according to your word"
(Luke 1:38, NRSV); "Your kingdom come. Your will be done, on
earth as it is in heaven" (Matthew 6:10, NRSV).

Fussing with the Bible. Sometimes praying the Bible
causes me to fuss with the Bible. Speaking to God with honesty
as well as reverence elicits protests. Listening to Jesus say, "Be
perfect" (Matthew 5:48), prompts me to respond, "Surely you're
kidding. I don't have a chance in the world of achieving perfection. Why set me up for failure?" This particular Scripture-cen-
tered prayer prods me to look more closely at the meaning of
Jesus' admonition. Eventually I discover that the word translated "perfect" means wholeness rather than flawless. Then, my
prayer of protest becomes a prayer of commitment, "I am trying
God. I long to be a whole person. Enable me to live with integrity
[another word for wholeness]—saying what I feel, meaning
what I say, practicing what I profess, behaving as I believe."

Another passage over which I invariably stumble comes from
one of the Epistles that bears the name of Peter. The writer said,
"Rejoice insofar as you are sharing Christ's sufferings" (1 Peter
4:13, NRSV). "I can't do that," I find myself whispering in
response, "I can't rejoice in my suffering for any reason." Once
I discover Peter's definition of joy and understanding of suffering, my prayer takes a different direction. I realize that the
inevitability of suffering in my life does not snuff out the possibility of joy. I speak to God with gratitude for a grace that may
be most illumined amid suffering.

Paul's words challenge and distress me as well as inspire and
encourage me. When the apostle declared, "I have learned to be
content with whatever I have" (Philippians 4:11, NRSV), I can

only respond with a prayerful confession and intention, "God, I'm not there. You know my impatience with things. But I am trying. With the aid of your Spirit, I want to move into the contentment voiced by brother Paul."

When the Bible has become an integral part of life—as a result of study and meditation—the Bible is a natural medium for conversations with God. Praying the Bible represents not borrowed words but offerings from the center of life. The Bible is a well from which Christian spirituality draws nourishment, a light from which it gains guidance, a promise from which it takes encouragement, and a strength from which it learns perseverance.

The Bible and Morality

A heated debate breaks out in a boardroom of a marketing agency. A major client has discovered a large run of inferior products. A decision must be made on whether to find a good way to sell bad merchandise or to admit the error in a manner that promotes the sale of the goods of low quality. A Christian executive quietly asks, "What *should* we do?"

Pained sighs accompany a recurring argument between a husband and wife. Conflict keeps ripping the relationship apart and leaving each partner weary and down. The husband suggests it may be best to give up on the marriage and separate. Then, he asks, "*Ought* we do that?"

Two teenagers feel besieged by a lethal combination of love, emotions, discipline, and hormones. The mixture takes a toll on moral convictions. "We can't go on like this," the young lady sighs, before asking, "What *should* we do?"

According to the Swiss theologian Emil Brunner, the question, What ought we to do? stands at the entrance to the Christian faith and constitutes the exit through which Christians move from the sanctuary of worship into life in the world. For most of us, personal experience corroborates that observation. Believing right is a snap compared to living right—making good decisions and engaging in moral actions.

Can the Bible aid moral decision making and ethical behavior? Some say no. Perhaps that is the reason for such a vast disparity between the popularity of the Bible and Bible-study groups and a decline in personal and social morality. Others, of whom I am one, argue to the contrary. Not only can the Bible assist people in moral dilemmas; the Bible should aid all committed to doing the will of God.

It is not easy, though. The Bible offers no specific guidance regarding many moral questions we must answer. In some instances, the Bible contains more than one perspective on the morality of a certain type of behavior. At points, different biblical texts contradict each other regarding an ethical concern. Even a person who sincerely wants to use the Bible as a moral compass can become confused and discouraged apart from understanding how the Bible helps in moral development and guidance. Keep in mind that the Bible is not a book of revealed morality but rather a book of the revelation of God. The Bible enables an understanding of God. Attempts to turn the Bible into a moral code book or a compendium of religious laws miss the point of the Bible's nature and value.

Moral responsibility involves much more than a mechanical application of rules to various situations followed by stoical obedience. The moral life consists of a personal response to God. Thoughtless compliance with ethical mandates requires little sense of responsibility, no volition, and minimal growth, if any at all. In sharp contrast to puppetlike obedience to rules, Christian morality is dynamic, imaginative, and creative— the result of meaningful communion with God. The Bible contributes inestimably to such morality and to the communion out of which it comes—guiding, encouraging, strengthening, enlightening, and inspiring us.

Biblical Foundations for Moral Decision Making

Biblical ethics are theological ethics. Responsible Christian morality reflects sound biblical theology. The Bible affirms three major convictions upon which a moral life securely rests.

Centrality of the Incarnation. The Word that became flesh continues to become flesh and dwell among us. The Bible introduces us to Jesus, who with one hand points to the path we should travel and with his other hand supports us as we go.

(This image borrowed from T. W. Manson continues to give me strength.) Jesus meets us in the same kinds of unlikely situations as those in which he appeared according to the New Testament records. Jesus offers to guide our resolution of daily moral dilemmas.

Cruciality of the church. God continues to work through the church, as flawed and weak as that body often appears. God provides the church with gifts of nurture, enlightenment, courage, and strength. Counsel and support from the church provide important encouragement and direction for moral decisions and actions.

Contemporaneity of the gospel. The gospel remains good news that inspires gratitude. The promise of the gospel frees us to take risks and even to fail in the process of doing good. Should we also fall short of the moral mark and sin against God, the gospel reminds us of a ready forgiveness. What comfort! Christian morality is a morality of gratitude and thanksgiving.

Biblical Principles for Moral Actions

Be careful here. The Bible contains a variety of ethical materials. However, the Bible is not a rule book or a code of ethics to which we can turn indiscriminately and promptly discover behavior to emulate or imperatives to obey. In fact, not all practices reported in the Bible fare well under the scrutiny of Christian morals.

Take family life, for example. Attempting to pattern a contemporary family after family models found in the Bible becomes a highly problematic enterprise. The Hebrew Scriptures laud as heroes and heroines of faith members of family units that most Christians consider immoral—families that included multiple wives, husbands with concubines, siblings at war with each other. Paul's recommendation that people marry only if they lack self-control (1 Corinthians 7:9) reflects anticipation of a quick end to history, not an ethic for durable relationships. Neither of these biblical perspectives on family life reflects the family values espoused by most Christians.

Consulting the Bible for moral guidance necessitates discretion.

Cultural norms and social mores differ dramatically from moral principles. We have no responsibility to reproduce life situations that stand outside the Christian tradition, even though they are reported in the Scriptures. Our interest focuses on the Bible's provision of basic moral principles that transcend specific periods of time and cultural biases to instruct decision making and action in every age. Here are three such principles of morality characteristic of Christian thoughts and actions.

Oriented to persons. Persons come first in Christian morality. This principle often enunciated by Jesus stirred up a sizable amount of controversy. When forced to choose between responding to pressing personal needs and complying with conflicting demands from religious institutions, Jesus consistently gave priority to helping persons. Jesus illustrated the primacy of persons as he spoke about the importance of sabbath observance, the fundamental institution in Judaism. "The sabbath was made for man," Jesus declared, "not man for the sabbath" (Mark 2:27). The Messiah took a similar position challenging people using the religious practice of "Corban" (a religious offering to God) to justify not providing financial support for their needy family members (Mark 7:11). Persons come first.

Centered on love. Jesus made no attempt to emulate Moses and establish a new body of moral laws. Over the whole course of his ministry, only once did Jesus institute a law at all: "This is my commandment, that you love one another as I have loved you" (John 15:12). Ironically the new law from Jesus made all other laws subservient to love.

Christian morality is motivated by love, centered on love, and demonstrative of love. Responsible morality refuses to violate the nature of Christian love. But what is the nature of this love? Jesus summed it up succinctly: "Greater love has no man than this, that a man lay down his life for his friends" (John 15:13). Paul's description of love involved more detail: "Love is patient and kind . . . not jealous or boastful . . . not arrogant or rude. Love does not insist on its own way; it is not irritable or resentful; it does not rejoice at wrong, but rejoices in the right. Love bears all things, believes all things, hopes all things, endures all things. Love never ends" (1 Corinthians 13:4-8).

Committed to Jesus Christ. Lewis Sheldon's classic novel

In His Steps suggested that every decision be made and every action taken after answering the question, "What would Jesus do?" Though simple to a fault, Sheldon's suggestion has merit. Christian morality takes all of its cues from the one whose name it bears and whose life it seeks to emulate. Decisions or actions that run contrary to the life and teachings of Christ have no place in Christian character.

The New Testament reports the teachings of Jesus and provides insights into the personal character and public ministry of Jesus. The morality incarnate in Christ is for all times, not just the time in which he lived. Jesus established standards and principles around which persons committed to the reign of God organize their lives. Jesus' morals are every bit as practical as they are radical. Christ's moral teachings make sense even though they require courageous obedience. Which is better—to forgive a person or to watch lingering ill will devastate a relationship? Does it make more sense to respond to evil in a manner that halts evil than to react to evil in a manner that perpetuates evil? The moral life commended and modeled by Jesus makes sense.

Beyond the Bible

The Bible alone is not enough to instruct and sustain a moral life. In some situations, the Bible simply does not provide us with enough information to make a definitive decision on the best course for moral action. Even then the Bible does not leave us hopeless. The Scriptures endorse other sources of moral insight to which we can turn for help.

Communal responsibility. Moral decision makers faithful to the biblical tradition inquire about the social consequences of a decision or action: How will my behavior affect other people? Will my action violate someone else's personhood, compromise his or her freedom, or result in injustice? A positive answer to the last question suggests restrictions related to the matter under consideration.

Common sense. God gave us minds to use. Revelation does not oppose reason. No act is more spiritual because it is irrational. In most instances, an action that fails to make good sense to a mind informed by Scripture also fails to qualify as morally responsible behavior.

The Holy Spirit. Christian morality involves an element of mystery. Sometimes a moral hunch arises from a mystical, inexplicable source. Such is the work of the Counselor, the Spirit of God promised by Jesus. Once we have done all we can do to decide a moral course of action, we hear the voice of God or feel the presence of God taking over the dilemma and guiding us through it.

Christian Formation

Moral demands seldom give us time to review our notes or consult legal codes. Usually we have to make a decision quickly, dependent only on the resources within us. That is why internalizing the moral principles of the Bible as well as incorporating the nature of God as revealed in the Bible is crucial.

The Bible's greatest contribution to the development of a moral life resides in its power to shape us as people of God. We live who we are. We act out our convictions. The Word becomes flesh in us and through us once more. Christian morality is inseparable from Christian spirituality. The Bible shapes both. As the mind of Christ takes form in us, we live *for* Christ and *as* christs in the world. We enjoy abundant life and find fulfillment in sharing this life with others. No wonder we bother with the Bible!